FOREORDAINED FAILURE

FOREORDAINED FAILURE

*The Quest for a
Constitutional Principle
of Religious Freedom*

STEVEN D. SMITH

OXFORD UNIVERSITY PRESS
New York   Oxford

Oxford University Press

Oxford   New York
Athens Auckland Bangkok Bogotá Buenos Aires Calcutta
Cape Town Chennai Dar es Salaam Delhi Florence Hong Kong Istanbul
Karachi Kuala Lumpur Madrid Melbourne Mexico City Mumbai
Nairobi Paris São Paulo Singapore Taipei Tokyo Toronto Warsaw

and associated companies in
Berlin Ibadan

First published in 1995 by Oxford University Press, Inc.
198 Madison Avenue, New York, New York 10016

First issued as an Oxford University Press paperback, 1999

Oxford is a registered trademark of Oxford University Press

Library of Congress Cataloging-in-Publication Data
Smith, Steven D. (Steven Douglas), 1952–
Foreordained failure : the quest for a constitutional principle of
religious freedom / Steven D. Smith.
p.   cm.
Includes bibliographical references and index.
ISBN 0-19-509075-6
ISBN 0-19-513248-3 (Pbk.)
1. Freedom of religion — United States.   2. Church and state —
United States.   3. United States — Constitutional law —
Amendments — 1st.   I. Title.
KF4783.S64 1994
342.73'0852 — dc20
[347.302852]   93-51041

1 3 5 7 9 8 6 4 2

Printed in the United States of America
on acid-free paper

PREFACE

Somewhat to my surprise, nearly everyone who read drafts of this book found it to be radical—"revolutionary," one reviewer said—but at the same time reticent. The book was radical, readers thought, because it seemed to argue that virtually all modern constitutional discourse on the subject of religious freedom is fundamentally misconceived. The book seemed reticent precisely because it declined to confess, or to work out the consequences of, its radicalism.

More specifically, several reviewers thought the claims made in the book extended well beyond the First Amendment's religion clauses. Those claims applied, some said, at least to the rest of the First Amendment—a better title for the book, my colleague Paul Campos suggested, would be "Honey, I Blew Up the First Amendment"—and perhaps to much else in constitutional law besides. So these reviewers wondered why I did not acknowledge, and perhaps explore, the broader reach of my arguments.

Even more commonly, reviewers wanted to know what normative consequences followed from my claims. If our current ways of talking about religious freedom under the Constitution do not make sense, then how *should* we talk about, and protect, religious freedom? More pointedly, what should courts do with the religion clauses?

These reactions prompt me to say something at the outset about what I conceive the purpose and scope of this book to be. It is hardly a novel observation that contemporary constitutional discourse on the subject of religious freedom is experiencing a kind of malaise. Virtually no one is happy with the Supreme Court's doctrines and decisions in this area or with its explanations of those doctrines and decisions. Many scholars and judges seem to believe, though, that this malaise can be cured by administering relatively mild remedies. If our historical research were just a little more careful (or less partisan), or if we could just replace the "purpose-effect-entanglement" test with a "coercion" test (or perhaps an "endorsement" test), *then* the discourse would become intelligible and the decisions defensible. Hence, a good deal of judicial and scholarly discussion is devoted to adjusting and tinkering and augmenting—to bolstering the historical case for one or another construction of the establishment or free exercise clause or to proposing a new doctrinal test or modification. Although even this discourse of adjustment can provoke strident disagreements, it is ultimately quite complacent about the possibilities and the general directions of the scholarly and judicial enterprise.

In earlier writings, I have contributed to this discourse of adjustment. I published an article criticizing the "endorsement" test, for example, and another article defending an "institutional separation" construction of the establishment clause. Over time, though, I came to sense the futility of this whole academic and judicial project. The entire body of modern constitutional discourse on the subject of religious freedom, I came to believe, was founded on empty premises and false assumptions. And if this was so, then there would be no cure for current frustrations from *within* the enterprise that judges and scholars have been pursuing.

What needed to be questioned and challenged, it seemed, was not the various particular views and conclusions that this enterprise has generated, but rather the enterprise itself, with its underlying assumptions and directions of inquiry. That is the critical challenge which this book tries to develop. Thus, I *am* arguing, as reviewers correctly understood, that virtually the whole of modern religion clause discourse is misconceived in its very foundations. In addition, I try to suggest some of the sources of our present predicament.

In trying to do this much, I am already asking readers to consider and accept—or, more accurately, give up—a lot. So there is neither need nor excuse, it seems to me, for making the argument any more expansive or demanding than it already is. Consequently, I am content for now to say that if readers believe the claims made here extend beyond the religion clauses, they may be right. Or perhaps not. Many of my arguments apply specifically to the religion clauses or to theories of religious freedom. But some of the arguments are not unique to the area of religion, and even those that are may have parallels in other areas. These possibilities raise interesting and important questions, but I think it would be premature, and foreign to my purpose, to try to resolve them here.

More readers will be frustrated, I suspect, by my failure to offer anything beyond general and very tentative suggestions regarding how we *should* talk—or about what the courts should do—about religious freedom. Contemporary legal scholarship, as my colleague Pierre Schlag has repeatedly argued, is pervasively normative; its analysis is typically oriented toward, and culminates in, some sort of prescription for the proper resolution (usually the proper *judicial* resolution) of the particular problem under consideration. The normative genre is so entrenched that a nonconforming piece of legal scholarship which fails to issue in such a prescription may leave readers feeling much the way detective-novel readers would feel if the story ended leaving the crime unsolved, or the way musicians are said to feel if someone plays the first seven notes of a major scale and then stops. Or readers may suspect that the author is being sneaky: He *must* be trying to advance *some* position, so why does he refuse to tell us what it is?

Although it is understandable that readers would like a more explicit normative conclusion, however, I respectfully submit that this expectation is unjustified and perhaps unhealthy. *Why* should legal scholarship have to conclude by prescribing what "we" (or the courts) should do? Scholarship in other disciplines does not invariably follow this pattern. And there are other functions that legal scholarship *can* perform, such as simply trying to illuminate our present situation. A strongly normative orientation can impede scholarship in its efforts to promote understanding by creating a perception—often enough an accurate one—that legal scholarship is really just disguised political advocacy. Moreover, the normative genre seems to reflect an immodest and unwarranted conception both of the importance of the individual author and, perhaps, of the importance of rationality and conscious decision in the governance of human affairs generally.

In this instance, the critical thesis developed in this book does not, so far as I can see, entail or logically generate any particular affirmative conclusions regarding the proper relationship between government and religion. So it seems to me better not to tack on gratuitous prescriptions. In any event, my normative views are so tentative, and perhaps ad hoc, that it would be difficult to elaborate them here even if I wanted to do so.

For anyone who may suspect some hidden agenda, I can frankly confess the attitudes that inform my normative opinions in this area. Perhaps because religious faith is central to my own life, I tend to disfavor governmental interference with religious activities and institutions. I am not sympathetic, for instance, to efforts to regulate religious institutions in the interest of achieving secular policy objectives. This disposition might incline me to favor aggressive judicial protection for religious freedom, at least for the autonomy of religious institutions. But that inclination is tempered in my case by the fact that I do not understand, or find plausible, the tremendous confidence that many legal scholars and political liberals generally seem to place in the wisdom and benevolence of the courts. So it is not as unthinkable for me as it may be for some legal scholars that the courts perhaps should simply withdraw from the business of trying to define and protect religious freedom. But to say that this possibility deserves serious, respectful consideration, as the final chapter suggests, is not to advocate such a course; and in fact I do not mean surreptitiously to advocate judicial withdrawal, as some reviewers seem to have believed. I mean no more than the final chapter says — that the possibility should not be regarded as beyond serious consideration.

Acknowledgments

A number of people helped me in the preparation of this book, and it would be impossible to list them all. Several friends and colleagues — Gerry Bradley, Paul Campos, Fred Gedicks, and Bob Nagel — generously read and commented on the entire book in an earlier version. Neal Devins, Alan Freeman, Kent Greenawalt, and Elizabeth Mensch kindly provided me with reviews that they did for publishers, and I also benefited from several other anonymous reviews done for publishers. Rick Collins and Gene Nichol gave valuable suggestions on a paper that evolved into chapters 2 through 4, and Rick's extensive historical knowledge has often been a help. Other friends, critics, and students too numerous to mention have helped me by discussing ideas and arguments made here or by commenting on articles, sections of which, in altered form, have become part of this book.

Finally, I thank my parents, my wife, Merina, and my children, Nathanael, Rachel, Maria, Jesse, and Christian, for their help and support. Their contribution to this book has been indirect but essential. None of them has read a word of the book. But they are, for me, presently visible manifestations of the love and goodness toward which religious faith and activity strive and thus the reason why the seemingly intractable problems of "religion," and hence of religious freedom, are worth struggling with.

It is probably apparent from what I have already said that my previous writing on the religion clauses could not be used intact in this book. But I have incorporated modified sections of earlier articles into the text in places, and I thank the following law reviews for permission to use these modified excerpts in this book.

"Moral Realism, Pluralistic Community, and the Judicial Imposition of Principle: A Comment on Perry." *Northwestern University Law Review*, Vol. 88 No. 1, pp. 183–192 (1993). Copyright 1993 by Northwestern University, School of Law, Northwestern University Law Review.

"The Rise and Fall of Religious Freedom in Constitutional Discourse." *University of Pennsylvania Law Review*, Vol. 140, No. 1, pp. 149–240 (1991). Copyright by the University of Pennsylvania.

"The Restoration of Tolerance." *California Law Review*, Vol. 78 No. 2, pp. 305–356 (1990). Copyright 1990 by California Law Review Inc.

"Separation and the "Secular": Reconstructing the Disestablishment Decision." 67 *Texas Law Review* 955 (1989). Copyright 1989 by the Texas Law Review Association. Reprinted by permission.

"Symbols, Perceptions, and Doctrinal Illusions: Establishment Neutrality and the "No Endorsement" Test." 86 *Michigan Law Review* 266 (1987). Copyright 1988 by The Michigan Law Review Association.

Boulder, Colorado   S.D.S.
October 1993

CONTENTS

FOREORDAINED FAILURE

1

Introduction: Rethinking "Rethinking Religious Liberty"

Although the need for "rethinking" something or other is a perennial theme in legal literature, calls for (and attempts at) rethinking religious liberty seem to have proliferated of late.[1] This development may or may not be wholesome, but it is hardly surprising. By the late 1980s it may have seemed that the constructions given by the Supreme Court to the religion clauses—to the clauses of the First Amendment which provide that "Congress shall make no law respecting an establishment of religion or prohibiting the free exercise thereof . . . "—had stabilized, for better or worse. Then, in 1990, the Court's decision in the "peyote case" upset what had been taken to be settled free exercise clause doctrine; in doing so, the decision also upset scores of commentators.[2] Two years later, the Court's decision in *Lee v. Weisman*, the graduation prayer case, left it unclear whether the Court's establishment clause doctrine, or the so-called *Lemon* test, still enjoyed the support of a majority of the justices.[3] Doctrinal changes seem in the offing, and such changes naturally provoke pleas for "rethinking."

These pleas would likely be forthcoming, however, even if the doctrine were more secure. In fact, even when the verbal formulations themselves seemed stable, the Court's religion clause doctrines seemed next to useless anyway. Douglas Laycock had described the Court's establishment clause formula as "so elastic in its application that it means everything and nothing."[4] John Mansfield's view was probably representative: The Court's religion clause decisions reflected "the incantation of verbal formulae devoid of explanatory value."[5]

Discontent at the level of doctrine has been matched by frustration on the level of results. The Court's 1984 decision approving a nativity scene in a Christmas display in Pawtucket, Rhode Island, provoked expressions of outrage by numerous commentators.[6] In a different vein, the increasingly conspicuous political presence of the religious Right in the 1980s and 1990s surely reflects a deepening conviction among some constituencies that judicial decisions prohibiting prayers at graduation ceremonies, invalidating "moment of silence" laws, and striking down laws providing for the "balanced treatment" of evolution and creationism in the public schools manifest a judicial determination to impose secularism on the schools, and hence on the next generation.[7] And in a time when concerns about education (and especially education for the disadvantaged) are high, it is understandable that the Court would produce dismay in some quarters when (on, what seemed to some, fanciful grounds) it invalidated remedial education programs that, as Justice Lewis F. Powell's concurring opinion conceded, had done "so much good and little, if any, detectable harm."[8] Both the Court's doctrine and its decisions, it may seem, have been disoriented and disorienting.

One diagnosis of these difficulties suggests that a half century ago the Supreme Court plunged into the turbulent waters of religious controversy without adequately considering either the historical meaning of the First Amendment's religion clauses or the practical consequences of judicial intervention. Mary Ann Glendon and Raul Yanes have recently contended for this view. Noting that the religion clauses were virtually dormant until the 1940s when the Supreme Court "incorporated" the clauses into the Fourteenth Amendment, Glendon and Yanes assert that "it is striking in retrospect to observe how little intellectual curiosity the members of the Court demonstrated in the challenge presented by the task of adapting, for application to the states, language that had long served to protect the states against the federal government."[9] Glendon and Yanes elaborate this criticism by examining several of the Court's decisions and then conclude:

> With hindsight, incorporation in the 1940s posed formidable legal-political challenges that should have called forth every ounce of energy, technical skill, and legal imagination available to the Court. Yet it is hard to escape the impression in reading the decisions of that era that — regardless of outcomes — serious issues were overlooked, important claims and arguments were rather

lightly dismissed, and practical implications for the lives of count-less Americans were regularly ignored. The Court skipped care-lessly over formidable problems of interpretation that required sustained attention to the language, history, and purposes of the original Constitution, Bill of Rights, the Fourteenth Amend-ment, and the relation among them in the modern regulatory state. [10]

This diagnosis easily leads to the conclusion that the serious thinking that was neglected earlier needs to be initiated now. Thus, like other scholars and critics, Glendon and Yanes hopefully call for "a long overdue reconsideration of Religion Clause jurisprudence from the foundations." [11]

What Is the Question?

It is difficult to disagree with the criticisms made by Glendon, Yanes, and others. Indeed, the Court's dismal historical perfor-mance in *Everson v. Board of Education*, [12] the first modern establish-ment clause case, and in later decisions has been persuasively dem-onstrated. [13] Thus, Michael Paulsen may be right in asserting that "[t]he Supreme Court's reading of the religion clauses is completely indefensible — historically, textually, and practically." [14] One may concede all of this, however, and still harbor doubts about the insis-tent call for "rethinking" religious liberty.

In alluding to "doubts," I mean nothing stronger than that. In an academic culture that purports to exalt thought and rationality, to oppose thinking or "rethinking" may be much like attacking a sacred icon. I do not mean, therefore, to argue against "rethinking," or to make the strong claim that "thinking" is in fact what brought us to our present predicament and that "rethinking" is only likely to aggravate the situation.

I do propose, however, that we might learn a useful lesson from the analytical philosophers: Thinking can be futile or worse — it can produce confusion rather than clarification — if the questions we think about are mistakenly or confusedly formulated. Hence, we need to be careful about how we frame our inquiries. It may be that the source of our present frustrations in the area of religious freedom is not that judges and scholars have given careless answers, but rather that they have asked wrong questions. If so, then no amount of rethinking, however meticulous or energetic, is likely to improve the situation as long as we insist on pressing the same bad questions.

I will argue in this book that this is just what has happened. Judges and constitutional scholars have been asking, in one form or another, something like the following question: "What is the meaning and scope of the principle of religious freedom embodied in the Constitution?" It is natural enough—indeed, it is probably inevitable—that judges and legal scholars would ask this question. Nonetheless, I will argue that the question in its various forms is a bad one; it is, and will remain, unanswerable on either historical or theoretical grounds. As long as our thinking focuses on this question, therefore, we are doomed to continuing frustration.

The Singular Conception of Religious Freedom

One consequence of the question just noted is that by quietly suggesting that religious freedom is something that can be reduced to or presented in the form of a "principle," the question may tempt us to think of religious freedom as if it were some singular ideal or state of affairs. This singular conception manifests itself in subtle ways. In everyday discourse, for example, we sometimes talk as if religious freedom were something that people can be, and often are, for or against. Roger Williams favored religious freedom, we may say, while the Puritan establishment in Massachusetts did not. Thomas Jefferson, but not Patrick Henry, supported religious freedom. This sort of "for or against" thinking is especially conspicuous in polemical periodicals like *Church and State*, published by Americans United for the Separation of Church and State. In that periodical, legal or political figures are regularly described as being for or against the separation of church and state, with ostensible opponents sometimes described as being in favor of "theocracy."[15]

The singular conception of religious freedom is also discernible in language implying that religious freedom is something that came into existence or that was adopted by one or another political institution at some particular point in time.[16] Virginia, it may be said, embraced religious freedom in 1786 when it enacted Jefferson's Virginia Statute for Religious Freedom, while Massachusetts did not adopt the principle of religious freedom until 1833 when it eliminated its religious establishment. Leo Pfeffer's "birth" metaphor typifies this view of religious freedom as something that comes into existence at a particular time: "The American principle of separation and religious liberty may then accurately be said to have been born in the last quarter century of the 18th century."[17]

Discussions of religious freedom in more academic legal literature are often more nuanced, yet at times this discourse also appears
to treat religious freedom as some singular and even objective ideal
that in some sense exists independently of people's opinions *about*
religious freedom. The singular conception is most clearly reflected
in a kind of argument commonly offered by legal scholars. The
argument asserts that some particular practice—legislative prayer,
for example, or governmental endorsement of religion—is and always has been inconsistent with the First Amendment even though
the framers of that amendment seem to have believed otherwise.
The reason this is so is that the framers adopted "the principle" of
religious freedom, or of church-state separation, and that principle
forbids legislative prayer or governmental endorsement of religion;
the framers of the amendment simply failed to recognize this. As
Douglas Laycock explains, "[t]he [constitutional] text states sweeping principles. . . . It is hardly surprising that the broad principles
stated in the text turn out to have implications that the founders did
not contemplate."[18] The same kind of argument is commonly used
by lawyers and judges.[19] It is hard to understand how this argument
could be plausible, or even intelligible, unless the principle of religious freedom is a self-subsisting ideal that is somehow independent
of the framers' thoughts and opinions about that principle. Conversely, if religious freedom *is* a singular and independent ideal,
then it is not surprising that the framers, or anyone else, might
endorse the principle of religious freedom without fully understanding the meaning or implications of that principle, in the same way
that I might buy a car or a computer without fully understanding
how these things work or what they are capable of doing.

In confronting actual human beings and political institutions,
this way of talking about religious freedom in the singular and as a
"for or against" matter can produce awkward interpretive problems.
Consider, for example, the Massachusetts Constitution of 1780. Article 2 expressly provided that "no subject shall be hurt, molested, or
restrained, in his person, liberty, or estate, for worshipping God in
the manner and season most agreeable to the dictates of his own
conscience."[20] Judging from this provision, one might infer that
the Massachusetts Constitution embraced religious freedom; and
indeed Massachusetts citizens and officials insisted that this was
so.[21] However, article 3 of that constitution went on to authorize
both taxation for the support of religion and compulsory attendance
at worship services.[22] Those provisions complicate the question. Did
the Massachusetts Constitution recognize religious freedom or not?

Or consider a curious statement made by Oliver Cromwell: "As to freedom of conscience, I meddle with no man's conscience; but if you mean by that, liberty to celebrate the mass, I would have you understand that in no place where the power of the Parliament of England prevails shall that be permitted."[23] Did Cromwell accept the principle of religious freedom?

Of course, similar apparent incongruities can be discerned in most — perhaps all — individuals and institutions. Thomas Aquinas argued that "the heathens and the Jews . . . are by no means to be compelled to the faith, . . . because to believe depends on the will." But he defended the use of physical compulsion against heretics and apostates.[24] Locke wrote stirringly in defense of religious toleration, but he explicitly excluded Muslims and atheists from the protection of that principle.[25] James Madison argued for religious freedom in his famous "Memorial and Remonstrance," and he helped secure the passage of Jefferson's monumental Virginia Statute for Religious Freedom. But on the same day on which he introduced that bill, Madison also sponsored a bill for punishing Sabbath breakers.[26] The First Congress approved the establishment and free exercise clauses, and at the same time it appointed legislative chaplains to begin each session with prayer and authorized a "day of public thanksgiving and prayer to be observed . . . [for] the many signal favors of Almighty God."[27]

Nor are seeming incongruities confined to the remote past. The modern Supreme Court announced a "wall between church and state" that is "high and impregnable" and not subject to "the slightest breach."[28] The Court then proceeded to allow some forms of aid to parochial schools, legislative prayer, the inclusion of a nativity scene in a public Christmas display, and the public funding of counseling activities by religious organizations.[29]

Ubiquitous Hypocrisy?

How should we regard these confusing, and seemingly confused, pronouncements and positions? Perhaps the most common response is to treat the incongruities as straightforward inconsistencies produced by lack of reflection, weakness of will, or simple hypocrisy. This sort of explanation is regularly advanced to explain the early Congress's apparent deviations from the principle of religious freedom that it is thought to have embodied in the religion clauses of the First Amendment. Religious freedom, the explanation goes, was a novel, unfamiliar principle, and it is hardly surprising that the framers of the religion clauses failed to think through all of its far-reaching implications.[30] Thus, when the framers approved legislative chaplains and thanksgiving proclamations, they were acting from "unreflective bigotry"[31] in violation of the principle they had just approved.

Similar explanations are given for the modern Supreme Court's vacillations with respect to the principle of "strict separation" announced in *Everson v. Board of Education*. In that case, Justice Robert H. Jackson condemned the Court's approval of a New Jersey program that subsidized the transportation of parochial school students by invoking a literary example of hypocrisy or weakness of will. "The case which irresistibly comes to mind as the most fitting precedent," Jackson observed, "is that of Julia who according to Byron's reports 'whispering "I will ne'er consent" — consented.'"[32] In a similar vein, commentators condemned the decision in *Lynch v. Donnelly* approving of a publicly sponsored nativity scene by asserting that the decision was not merely legally incorrect but also "disingenuous" and "sleazy,"[33] or "wholly unprincipled."[34]

This approach to apparent incongruities would allow us to preserve the conceit of religious freedom as a singular ideal, with the associated assumption that individuals can be for or against religious freedom, by assigning persons to either of two categories. One category would include people who really do or did favor religious freedom, even though thoughtlessness or "unreflective bigotry" may occasionally have led them to depart from this principle. Most scholars would probably place the framers of the religion clauses on this list. The modern Supreme Court, or at least some of its members such as Justices William J. Brennan, Jr., and Hugo L. Black, might also be counted as favoring religious freedom — albeit with occasional lapses. So, probably, would Locke, although his exceptions for atheists and Muslims might make his case more controversial.

The second category would contain individuals who did *not* genuinely believe in the principle of religious freedom, even though through simple inconsistency or for political reasons they sometimes said they did. Aquinas, Oliver Cromwell, and the framers of the Massachusetts Constitution of 1780 would likely be placed on this list. Some current justices — Chief Justice William H. Rehnquist, perhaps, or Justice Antonin Scalia[35] — might also be assigned to this category.

Given the prevalence of human thoughtlessness and hypocrisy, this way of dealing with complex cases has some plausibility. In addition, the approach fits nicely with deep-seated notions about progress and evolving enlightenment — with a pervasive "conception of human history as a single universal process of struggle towards the light, the later stages and embodiments of which are necessarily superior to the earlier."[36] By this view, the history of Western thought and politics in this area represents the gradual unfolding or the progressive realization of a grand political idea. The germ of religious freedom — of *the* ideal or principle of religious freedom — is already discernible in ancient and medieval times, although because of shortsightedness or lack of commitment or both, rulers and thinkers of those periods did not go very far with the notion. In this vein, John Noonan asserts that Thomas Aquinas's views about the sanctity of conscience "carried the seed of religious liberty" but that this seed did not bear fruit until much later.[37] Although there were in Aquinas's medieval heritage "venerable teachers . . . that pointed to more merciful and more magnanimous conclusions," Aquinas failed to draw those conclusions because for him "[p]ractice was decisive. In the world Thomas knew, heretics were sent to the flames."[38]

Later, political philosophers like Locke advanced the development of the principle, but the very familiarity of intolerance in their times blinded them to the principle's full implications.[39] The framers of the Constitution went farther still, although entrenched customs and practices such as legislative prayer continued to cloud their vision or undermine their commitment.[40] Hence, it has been left to modern judges and scholars to carry on and perhaps complete the task by working out, and then working into the law, the full meaning of the principle of religious freedom.

This depiction is, to be sure, a pleasing one — and one that contemporary judges and scholars would naturally find flattering and invigorating. Still, there is something troubling, and more than a little presumptuous, in a viewpoint that is forced to classify virtually everyone who came before us, as well as most of our contemporaries, as lacking in reflection, or weak-willed, or hypocritical. At least some of the figures so classified — Aquinas, for example, or Madison — seem not to have been discernibly less reflective, or more morally compromised, than the modern scholars who casually explain away their presumed failings in this fashion.

A principle of charity in interpretation, or even of ordinary modesty, might suggest that we not rely so heavily on imputed thoughtlessness or hypocrisy if there is any plausible alternative. But *is* there in fact any other way of accounting for the seeming incongruities in the various positions that have been taken with regard to religious freedom?

The Varieties of Religious Freedom

When the question is posed in this way, at least one alternative seems clear. We might simply relinquish the singular conception of religious freedom and admit that there are potentially many versions of religious freedom. To put it differently, we might acknowledge that there is no single or self-subsisting "principle" of religious freedom; there is only a host of individuals with a host of different opinions and notions about how much and what kind of scope government ought to give to the exercise of religious beliefs and practices. [41] Aquinas's views on this subject were different from Cromwell's; Cromwell's were different from Madison's. But all these figures believed in *some* version of religious freedom; they believed, that is, in giving some scope to divergent religious beliefs or practices. And it is simply misleading to suppose that there is a univocal principle of religious freedom, hovering in some Platonic realm independent of these different opinions—a principle of which the opinions of Aquinas, Cromwell, and Madison were more or less faithful copies.

It is important to clarify how this more pluralistic approach to the question differs from an approach that at least tacitly conceives of religious freedom as a unitary principle or a singular ideal. In acknowledging a variety of versions of religious freedom, we can still insist that some opinions about the proper scope of religious freedom are more attractive, or more rationally defensible, than others. I might believe, for example, that the arguments for the positions I take on the issues of religious freedom are more persuasive than the arguments for the positions taken by Cromwell—or Justice Brennan. This disagreement, however, merely entails the familiar sort of debate about whose arguments are stronger or whose position is more attractive or plausible. There is little to be gained by trying to frame the debate as one about who really perceives the true meaning of "the principle of religious freedom." Consequently, although I might assert that those who disagree with me are "wrong" or that their arguments are "weak" or "implausible," I would have no justification at all for saying, for example, that they have failed to understand the very principle that they purport to respect or that in professing to respect that principle they are being thoughtless or hypocritical.

Likewise, a more pluralistic approach to religious freedom would not prevent us from discerning in Western history a kind of progress toward the achievement of more complete religious freedom. This characterization might simply mean that current notions of religious freedom allow greater scope for diverse religious conduct and belief. It might also mean that we think the reasons supporting current opinions are more plausible than those invoked in behalf of earlier views. Conversely, it is unnecessary and potentially misleading to say that "the principle" of religious freedom was somehow implicit in but inadequately expressed by earlier positions, or that Western history reflects an ongoing, ever more perfect realization of *the* principle of religious freedom.

In short, the pluralistic approach allows us to say much of what we already say about religious freedom but denies any self-subsisting status to "the principle" of religious freedom. There is, consequently, no unitary principle of religious freedom; rather there are numerous versions of religious freedom, which may be more or less attractive and defensible. Nearly everyone will believe, sincerely, in *some* version of religious freedom. The interesting question, consequently, is not whether I, or Justice Scalia, or Cromwell, or anyone else is or was "for or against" religious freedom. The descriptive question, rather, is which version of religious freedom a person believes in, and the normative question is which version of religious freedom is most attractive or sound, either generally or in a given context.

The Constraints of Judicial Review

The pluralistic approach to religious freedom seems both more charitable and more metaphysically frugal than the unitary approach. Nonetheless, the pluralistic approach poses difficulties that may make it unappealing to constitutional lawyers and scholars. One difficulty is that the pluralistic approach undermines a favorite lawyerly and scholarly argument. The pluralistic approach makes problematic, that is, the kind of argument that claims that a particular conclusion is required by "the principle" adopted by the framers even though the framers seem not to have accepted that conclusion. [42]

More generally, constitutional discourse is concerned — some might say obsessed — with judicial review. When constitutional lawyers and scholars address issues like religious freedom, they are interested in generating theories or principles that can be embodied in fairly simple doctrinal formulations that can in turn be used by courts in assessing and sometimes invalidating controversial laws and practices. [43] Abandoning the unitary conception might complicate this task. Suppose, for example, that so-called Christian Reconstructionists somehow manage to take temporary control of politics in California, and they adopt a provision (similar to those that existed in many states in the early years of the Republic) prohibiting non-Protestants from holding state public office. A group of Catholics, Muslims, Jews, and agnostics challenges this law under the religion clauses of the First Amendment. Assuming a unitary conception of religious freedom simplifies the court's task and permits a decision that will be almost syllogistic in its force. The court need merely say: (1) the First Amendment adopts the principle of religious freedom; (2) a law imposing religious qualifications for public office violates that principle (whether or not the constitutional framers understood this); (3) therefore, the California law, by imposing religious qualifications, violates the First Amendment.

From a pluralistic perspective, by contrast, the problem is more complicated. Now it is understood that there is no single theory or principle of religious freedom. Hence, the Reconstructionists might make the following argument: "The Constitution approves of religious freedom, and so do we. But of course there are many versions of religious freedom. We in California happen to favor the Oliver Cromwell version. And as long as we adhere to *a* version of religious freedom, we have not violated the Constitution."

Of course, the Reconstructionists' argument is far from invincible. The instinctive response of judges and lawyers would assert that even if the Cromwell position can be considered *a* genuine version of religious freedom, it is incompatible with *the Constitution's version*; hence, the California law is still unconstitutional. This answer creates a new difficulty, though: How do we know which among the various versions of religious freedom *is* "the Constitution's version"?

As long as we indulge the unitary conception of religious freedom, this question poses no great difficulty. If religious freedom constitutes a singular ideal or unitary principle, then that ideal or principle is the Constitution's version because there is no other (although there may be many conflicting opinions, most of them of necessity mistaken, about the ideal or principle). To talk about "the Constitution's version" of religious freedom is simply to talk about the "true" principle of religious freedom; finding the Constitution's version merely involves discerning *the* principle from among the many impostors. But once we acknowledge that there are many versions of religious freedom and that these are indeed genuine versions, the matter becomes more complicated. How *do* we know whether Cromwell's views, or Justice Scalia's, or Justice Brennan's correspond to "the Constitution's version"? Indeed, what does it even mean to say that version *X* is "the Constitution's version" but version *Y* is not?

Two Roads to "the Constitution's Version"

Perhaps the easiest answer, if it were available, would be that the words used in the Constitution explicitly and unequivocally adopt a particular version of religious freedom. Unfortunately, for most controversies this answer is simply not plausible. Scholars and judges have squeezed and tortured the words of the religion clauses for all the meanings those words can give, but those meanings remain meager and, usually, controversial. Typically, therefore, scholars and judges have resorted to either of two other approaches — we may call them the "originalist" and the "theoretical" approaches — in an effort to discern *the Constitution's* theory or principle of religious freedom.

The "originalist" approach holds that the Constitution's version of religious freedom is the one that its framers and ratifiers intended to adopt. A good deal of case law and modern legal scholarship has proceeded from this assumption. In its first modern establishment clause decision, *Everson v. Board of Education*,[44] the Supreme Court purported to ascertain and apply the original meaning of that clause. Friends of *Everson*'s "separationist" construction have tried to buttress that position with more extensive historical argumentation,[45] while critics of *Everson* have responded in kind, attacking the separationist position on historical grounds.[46] More recently, constitutional scholars have begun to give careful attention to the question of original meaning with respect to the free exercise clause as well.[47] After almost half a century, and despite exaggerated predictions of its demise,[48] this debate shows no signs of disappearing: Recently, in *Lee v. Weisman*, Justice David H. Souter entered the establishment clause debate by offering his own exposition of the original meaning.[49]

The theoretical approach, by contrast, does not assume that the Constitution's version of religious freedom was fixed by human intentions at the time of the First Amendment's enactment. Instead, this approach seeks to articulate the best, or the most plausible, or the most theoretically attractive version of religious freedom.

Scholarship in this vein is also plentiful. Such scholarship concentrates less on historical evidence and more on political philosophy or on contemporary policy justifications.

In actuality, most modern scholarship mixes the originalist and theoretical approaches. Even self-avowed originalists will generally concede that historical inquiry does not yield specific answers to concrete legal questions. Instead, the originalist scholar seeks to extract from the historical materials a "principle" that requires analysis and elaboration before it can be applied to current controversies. [50] Conversely, scholars of a more theoretical bent typically assert, or at least assume, that their theories are in some sense rooted in the original decision expressed in the religion clauses. Without this assumption, it would be unclear how their theories could be considered "constitutional" theories at all. [51]

Misguiding Questions

Earlier I asserted that judges and constitutional scholars have been asking, in one form or another, the following question: What is the meaning and scope of the principle of religious freedom embodied in the Constitution? We can now see that this basic question may appear in different forms. Judicial opinions and legal scholarship sometimes seem to treat religious freedom as a unitary conception; hence, to ask "What principle of religious freedom does the Constitution adopt?" is equivalent to asking "What is the real meaning of religious freedom?"

In other moods, however, legal discourse recognizes that there are different versions of religious freedom. [52] In that case, the relevant question seems to be this: Which *version* of religious freedom does the Constitution adopt? And that question, in turn, is usually understood in either (or both) of two ways. The question may be understood as a question about the original meaning of the religion clauses. Conversely, the basic question may be understood as asking, What is the best or the most plausible theory of religious freedom?

Although both the originalist and theoretical forms of the inquiry are natural and familiar, I will argue in this book that both present unanswerable questions. Chapters 2 through 4 argue that the originalist approach is foreordained to failure. Some readers will be predisposed to accept this conclusion on general grounds; they may assume that historical inquiry is never capable of generating any "original understanding" that would be useful today in deciding concrete cases. My own argument is in a sense just the opposite of this familiar view, and is more specific to the religion clauses. I maintain that we *can* ascertain the probable original meaning of those clauses, and when we do we also discover, paradoxically, that the religion clauses have nothing of substance to say on questions of religious freedom. The original meaning supplies us neither with concrete answers to particular legal questions nor with any general principle, norm, value, or theory that might serve as a basis for working out such answers.

Readers who are already disposed to accept the futility of the originalist approach, whether for the reasons given here or because of the more familiar objections to originalism, might skip these chapters and go directly to chapters 5 through 8, which adopt a very different tone and focus. In those chapters, I argue against the possibility of any adequate general theory of religious freedom. My thesis in this part of the book is that religious freedom, like many other matters of both personal and political concern, is inherently a prudential matter that cannot plausibly be confined to or regulated by "theory." Moreover, theoretical reflection cannot vindicate the position of "neutrality" that judges and scholars have struggled to define but instead shows that position to be illusory. Consequently, insofar as scholars seek to derive the Constitution's principle of religious freedom from political or legal theory, they are consigned to continuing frustration.

This analysis both supports and casts doubt on the insistent demand noted at the beginning of this chapter — the demand for rethinking religious liberty. It is true that current understandings and formulations of religious freedom give no cause for contentment. Indeed, if one spends a little time studying current doctrine and decisions, the need for rethinking may seem urgent. But if our present unsatisfactory condition is the product of inquiries and ways of thinking that were doomed from the start, then merely pursuing *those* inquiries and persisting more assiduously in *those* ways of thinking will only preserve, and perhaps even aggravate, our current confusion. In attempting to show how failed efforts have resulted from faulty questions, this book seeks to clear away obstructions and thereby, perhaps, to open up the possibility of thinking and talking about religious freedom in more fruitful ways.

2

The Jurisdictional Character of the Religion Clauses

In this chapter I will argue that an originalist approach to the religion clauses tells us nothing about the substantive meaning of religious freedom. My argument does not rely on standard objections to originalist interpretation that emphasize the indeterminacy of the constitutional text or the conundrums that plague the concept of "framers' intent."[1] The reason why the originalist approach provides no assistance with respect to the legal content of religious freedom, I will argue, is *not* that we cannot ascertain the original meaning of the religion clauses. On the contrary, we *can* discern what was probably their essential meaning, and when we do so we discover that the religion clauses were purely jurisdictional in nature; they did not adopt any substantive right or principle of religious freedom.

This conclusion is not based on any newly discovered historical evidence or on any novel method of textual interpretation. Rather, the conclusion results from working out the implications of historical facts that are already familiar to and widely accepted by scholars interested in this area. I emphasize that I will not rely, in the next few chapters, on any evidence that is not well known, and indeed readily accessible not only in primary sources but also in a number of secondary works to be found in most academic libraries. My purpose is simply to face up more fully than most judges and scholars have done to the implications of that evidence — implications that I believe are plausible and even compelling once we clear away the

17

misformulated inquiries that have caused us to overlook, or at least fail to appreciate, the obvious.

The Religion Clauses in a Federalist Framework

The analysis begins with a commonplace: The religion clauses, as understood by those who drafted, proposed, and ratified them, were an exercise in federalism. First Amendment scholars have often noted the federalist element in the religion clauses, particularly in the establishment clause,[2] and have realized that this element poses difficulties, both historical and conceptual, for the theory that the establishment clause was "incorporated" into the Fourteenth Amendment and thereby extended to the states.[3]

This acknowledgment, however, has had little discernible effect on legal discourse about the meaning of the religion clauses. Judges and scholars have assumed that the religion clauses contain both a federalist element and a substantive principle or right and that their substantive content can be extracted and elaborated independently of the clauses' federalism. This dualistic view of the religion clauses became dominant almost as soon as the clauses had been "incorporated." One of the early scholars in the post-*Everson* period to address the subject, Joseph Snee, maintained that "[t]he First Amendment . . . is not only an express guarantee of personal religious freedom against the threat of federal action, but also an application of the principle of federalism. *The two purposes must be clearly and unequivocally distinguished.*"[4] Mark Dewolfe Howe's classic *The Garden and the Wilderness* also adopted this dualistic view of the religion clauses. Howe's was a leading study that emphasized the predominantly federalist character of the establishment clause. His conclusion, however, that "the federalism of the First Amendment may be even more important than its libertarianism,"[5] clearly implied that the religion clauses had, in addition to their federalist component, a substantive or "libertarian" element. Not surprisingly, therefore, later scholars have admired Howe's study,[6] without feeling in the least deterred from elaborating the substantive principles or rights that they believe the religion clauses to contain.

I will argue that this dualistic view of the religion clauses, although virtually ubiquitous, is nonetheless mistaken. The religion clauses were not a hybrid creation—part federalism, part substantive right. They were, rather, simply an assignment of jurisdiction over matters of religion to the states—no more, no less. Consequently, perverse though it seems, the religion clauses simply do not speak to the substantive questions of religious freedom.

The following discussion begins by laying out the basic argument for the jurisdictional construction of the religion clauses. It then considers a number of complications and possible objections.

The "Religion Question" and the "Jurisdiction Question"

The original meaning of the religion clauses must be sought, of course, in the political and religious context that generated them. In the newly organized nation, issues of religious freedom generated distinct questions. One kind of question may be thought of as first-order or substantive: This was the question of the proper relationship between government and religion. Should government establish one religion as the official state religion? Should the state subsidize a religion? Should it support all religions, or at least all Protestant religions, on equal terms? Should religious heresy or blasphemy be punished? Should conventional religious practices—Sabbath observance, for example—be enforced by law? For present purposes, these and similar issues may be grouped under the general heading of the "religion question."

A second-order question was one of governmental organization, or of the allocation of jurisdiction. Which level of government, state or national, should be responsible for addressing the first-order question? This second-order issue presented the "jurisdiction question."

With respect to the first-order or religion question, views in the new nation were of course diverse; but most of the then prevailing opinions can be assigned to two, or perhaps three, broad positions. The first position, and the one supported by received wisdom and tradition, can be described in two claims or propositions. First, religion is essential to a stable social and political order. Second, governmental support is needed to maintain this essential religious foundation. The traditional position had been almost universally held in Western societies for centuries,[7] and it enjoyed widespread support in this country.[8] It was embodied in article 3 of the Massachusetts Constitution of 1780:

> As the happiness of a people, and the good order and preservation of civil government, essentially depend upon piety, religion, and morality: and as these cannot be generally diffused through a Community, but by the institution of the public worship of God,

and of public instructions in piety, religion, and morality: Therefore to promote their happiness and to secure the good order and
preservation of their government, the people of this Commonwealth have a right to invest the Legislature [with authority to
provide for mandatory church attendance and support of
churches from public funds].[9]

Years after the adoption of the religion clauses, the traditional
view still retained its appeal in some quarters. For example, Yale
president Timothy Dwight argued for a state-established religion in
just these terms: "[N]o free government has ever existed for any
time without the support of religion. . . . But religion cannot exist,
and has never existed for any length of time, without public worship."[10]

A second emerging view may be called the "voluntarist" position. This view accepted the first but not the second of the claims
associated with the traditional position; it agreed that a religious
foundation was vital to the political and social order, but it insisted
that governmental support was not essential, and indeed might well
be harmful, to the cause of religion. This voluntarist view was characteristic not only of dissenting religious groups, such as the Baptists, but also of "enlightened" statesmen, such as Jefferson and
Madison (at least in their public pronouncements).[11]

Whether any significant body of opinion rejected *both* of the
traditional position's claims is less clear. Although Jefferson sometimes asserted the public necessity of religion,[12] skeptics have long
suspected that his secret intent in promoting religious freedom was
to undermine traditional Christianity. Robert Baird, the nine-
teenth-century religious historian, believed that Jefferson was "a
very bitter enemy to Christianity, and we may even assume that he
wished to see not only the Episcopal church separated from the state
in Virginia, but the utter overthrow of everything in the shape of a
church throughout the country."[13] With respect to Jefferson's famous Virginia Statute for Religious Freedom, Baird opined that
"it gave its author great satisfaction, not because it embodied the
principles of eternal justice, but because by putting all religious sects
on an equality, it seemed to degrade Christianity. . . . It was this
that made the arch-infidel chuckle with satisfaction."[14] If this suspicion is correct, then Americans like Jefferson may have embraced a
third position, which may aptly be called a "heretical" view both
because it broadly rejected the prevailing orthodoxy and because its
proponents seem to have found it prudent to be discreet about their
actual opinions.[15]

Even if the heretical position is disregarded, however, the difference between the traditional and the voluntarist positions was significant. Despite their shared first premise, their divergence on the second traditional claim meant that these positions disagreed at a fundamental level over the proper relationship between government and religion: The traditional position regarded governmental support for religion as essential to the social order, while the voluntarist position opposed such support. How then were proponents of these conflicting positions able to agree on an answer to the religion question in adopting a constitutional provision on the subject?

The answer is that they did *not* agree; instead, they chose in effect to avoid answering the first-order question by leaving it to the states. The religion clauses kept the national government out of religion not because governmental support for religion was generally regarded as improper — *that* was precisely the issue on which the traditional and voluntarist positions divided — but rather because the religion question was within the jurisdiction of the states. Thus, voluntarists could support the religion clauses because they permitted states to adopt a voluntarist position, as Virginia had recently done. Traditionalists could support the amendment precisely because it prohibited the national government from interfering with states like Massachusetts and Connecticut that adhered to the traditional position favoring established religion. [16]

If we ask, therefore, what principle or theory of religious liberty the framers and ratifiers of the religion clauses adopted, the most accurate answer is "None." They consciously chose not to answer the religion question, and they were able for the most part to avoid it (or at least they thought they were) because of the way in which they answered the jurisdiction question — that is, by assigning the religion question to the states. This observation suggests that it is futile to try to extrapolate or reconstruct a principle or theory of religious liberty from the original meaning of the religion clauses. Those clauses quite simply were not based on any such principle or theory.

Daniel Conkle makes just this point, although only with respect to the establishment clause:

> Given this widespread and deep division, how could Congress and the ratifying state legislatures have reached agreement on the establishment clause? It was supported, after all, both by separationists and by those who were committed to programs of state-sponsored religion. These various political actors simply could not have agreed on a general principle governing the rela-

tionship of religion and government, whether it be the principle endorsed in *Everson* or any other. If the establishment clause had embraced such a principle, it would not have been enacted. What united the legislatures was a much more narrow purpose: to make it plain that *Congress* was not to legislate on the subject of religion, thereby leaving the matter of church-state relations to the individual states. This purpose honored the anti-establishment policies of states such as Virginia, but it also protected the existing state establishments from congressional interference.[17]

Conkle is neither the first nor the last scholar to reach this conclusion with respect to the establishment clause.[18] Nonetheless, arguments like Conkle's do not seem to have affected scholarly or judicial theorizing about the religion clauses in any discernible way. Perhaps the project of reading substantive meaning into the religion clauses has gained so much momentum that no scholarly argument, no matter how persuasive, could inhibit it. On the other hand, it may be that judges and scholars are simply not convinced. And in fact there *are* possible objections to the construction advocated by Conkle. The following discussion considers some of those objections and seeks to make the jurisdictional construction more secure.

In addition, a few scholars, while conceding that the *establishment clause* did not adopt any substantive principles or rights, have contended that the *free exercise clause* does reflect a substantive commitment to rights of religious freedom. The next chapter addresses that claim.

The Substance of the Religion Clauses' Federalism

The original federalist character of the religion clauses, and indeed of the Bill of Rights generally,[19] is widely acknowledged. But a measure can have a federalist component — it can apply to the national government but not to the states — and in addition adopt a substantive principle or enact a substantive right — albeit one applicable only to the national government. The Eighth Amendment's prohibition on cruel and unusual punishment seems a case in point: The prohibition may not initially have applied to the states, but it nonetheless seems to have limited the national government in accordance with a substantive right or principle disfavoring inhumane punishment. The religion clauses, similarly, might have applied only to the national government and yet have embodied a substantive principle or right of religious freedom.

Indeed, it seems undeniable that the religion clauses *did* have substantive content. Those clauses surely prevented the national government from establishing an official national church, for example, or from doing whatever amounted to "prohibiting the free exercise [of religion]." These observations may suggest that the course judges and constitutional scholars have typically followed is perfectly sensible: that is, acknowledge that the religion clauses had a federalist component, point out that this component has been rendered largely obsolete by the "incorporation" of the First Amendment into the Fourteenth, and then proceed to elucidate the enduring substantive meaning of those clauses.

In considering this possibility, it is helpful at the outset if we distinguish between two varieties of federalism, which might be called "federalism as a side constraint" and "essential federalism." Consider two different situations in which a national institution might adopt a federalist position regarding a particular matter. In one situation, a national institution—Congress, say, or a constitutional convention—might be presented with a substantive issue, such as the legitimacy of slavery; and the national delegates might reach a consensus regarding the proper resolution of that issue. They might conclude, let us suppose, that slavery is deeply immoral and that it should be forbidden. Despite this consensus, the national institution might nonetheless be constrained in ways that cause it to refrain from imposing its position on the states, even though it may hope the states will embrace the same position. For instance, the national institution might simply lack the power to impose its solution on the states. Or the imposition of that solution might be too costly. Or the national institution might for independent reasons regard state autonomy as an important value in itself—one which outweighs the value of achieving a specific policy goal favored by the national institution. For any of these reasons, a national institution conceivably might opt for a federalist position on the issue. In this situation, federalism would act as an obstacle or side constraint that inhibits the national institution from fully implementing its preferred policy or program.

In a different situation, a national institution might choose federalism in a more affirmative way. Suppose that a bill is introduced in Congress that would require all public secondary schools to provide mandatory instruction on AIDS and the use of safe contraceptive methods. Perhaps Congress can reach no agreement on this issue. Or the legislators, while sharing a tentative opinion, might also distrust their own judgment; they might think that someone else — state or local officials, perhaps — understands matters of school curriculum better than they themselves do, or that in matters of this kind it is most desirable to let states and localities function as "laboratories." These considerations might lead Congress to adopt a more positive version of federalism. In this positive version, state or local control over an issue is not an obstacle to or limitation on the achievement of any national policy. On the contrary, the only relevant national policy is precisely that of leaving the issue to state or local control. Federalism, in short, is not a mere "side constraint"; it is the essence of national policy on this issue.

If a national institution affirmatively adopts a substantive principle or policy but because of federalist side constraints refrains from imposing it on the states, then the substantive meaning of the principle or policy is independent of the constraints that limit its application. Consequently, if these side constraints lose their force, nothing impedes the extension of the principle or policy to the states. That possibility seems available, for example, in the case of the prohibition of cruel and unusual punishment. The substantive meaning of that prohibition may be murky, but it does not seem to hinge on whether the prohibition applies to the national government only or to the state governments as well.

Conversely, it seems nonsensical or incoherent to suggest that a provision representing "essential federalism" has a substantive meaning independent of its federalism or that the provision has substantive content that can be "extended" to the states. Suppose, for example, that after considering various questions of school curriculum, Congress concludes that these questions should all be resolved on the state and local levels and accordingly enacts a law that provides: "Matters of school curriculum shall be within the sole jurisdiction of the states; and no institution or agency of the national government shall interfere with or attempt to influence the exercise of that jurisdiction by the states." In this instance, federalism is not a side constraint on the law but rather its essence; the law has no substantive meaning independent of its federalism. Hence, a suggestion at some later date that the provision should be "extended" to the states would be nonsensical. What could such a suggestion even mean? The provision might of course be revised or repealed, but in its original form it already "extends" to the states in the only sense that it could apply to them.

With respect to any particular federalist measure, therefore, such as the religion clauses, we may properly ask whether the measure's federalism represents the essence of the measure or a mere side constraint qualifying the scope of a substantive national program or policy. In this context, however, the word *substantive* may mislead, and it is therefore necessary to notice a conceptual trap that is likely to catch the careless scholar or judge. In deciding which kind of federalism a measure reflects, it is not sufficient to note that the measure has "substantive" content or that it imposes "substantive" restrictions on government by, for example, prohibiting the national government from regulating certain subjects or from enacting certain kinds of laws. Both types of federalist measures will necessarily have substantive content or impose substantive restrictions. One kind of measure adopts a substantive right, policy, or principle and, in addition, adopts a federalist limitation that *qualifies or restricts* the reach of that substantive right, policy, or principle. The other kind of measure imposes a substantive restriction on one level or branch of government as a means of assigning jurisdiction over a subject-matter to another level or branch of government.

Thus, a purely federalist decision in effect defines certain substantive domains or subject-matter areas in order to assign them to the jurisdiction of one level of government rather than to another. It does not follow, however, that the measure supplies or implies any answer to the "substantive" questions that arise within those domains. On the contrary, the measure's substantive provisions are calculated *not* to answer such questions, but merely to specify *who* (or *what level of government*) shall answer them.

For example, the hypothetical law on school curricula described earlier affirmatively restricts national agencies from making decisions regarding school curricula. That restriction is "substantive" in a sense, but it merely ensures that curricular decisions will be made by the states; the restriction in no way reflects a decision or principle that curricular decisions should not be made at all, or that *government* (state or national) should not decide issues of school curricula. Hence, a later judicial decision forbidding states and localities to decide such issues would not be an "extension," logical or otherwise, of the original provision, or of the "principle" of that provision; on the contrary, such a decision would be a repudiation of the provision.

The point can be put more abstractly: The proposition "I should not do *X because* it is *your* responsibility to do *X*" does not in any way lead to or support the proposition "*X* should not be done" (with its logical corollary "*You* should not do *X*"). The latter proposition and its corollary do not extend or supplement the former proposition, but rather negate it.

In considering the religion clauses, therefore, the observation that those clauses contain substantive language and substantive content does not by itself offer any basis for determining which kind of federalism the clauses reflect. The question is not whether the clauses imposed substantive restrictions on the national government — plainly, inevitably, they did — but instead whether these restrictions were adopted to effect a positive national policy on the subject of religious freedom or, more modestly, were calculated merely to assign jurisdiction over matters of religion to the states. [20]

Which Kind of Federalism?

Two considerations argue forcefully, I think, for the conclusion that the framers and ratifiers chose to avoid the first-order or religion question altogether and consequently adopted an essentially federalist measure, rather than adopting a positive position on the religion question subject to a federalist side constraint. Perhaps the most important argument has already been noted: The founders *did not* answer the religion question because they *could not* have done so. The differences between the traditional and voluntarist positions, both of which enjoyed significant support, meant that Americans in the late eighteenth century held contradictory positions at a basic level regarding the religion question. One position saw governmental support for religion as permissible, and even essential, while the other position strenuously objected to such support. In this context, it is hard to see how the founding generation could have agreed on any substantive answer to the religion question. And even more than "ought implies can," "could not" implies "did not."

In an oblique way, the records of discussion in the First Congress provide a second cogent (albeit generally overlooked) argument for the view that the framers did not attempt to answer the religion question. Congressional discussions of the religion clauses were, as judges and scholars have sometimes lamented, desultory and superficial. [21] Most state ratifying conventions approved the measure with even less reflection or discussion. [22] This apparent complacency may seem not only unfortunate but also puzzling. The paucity of discussion plainly did not reflect any incapacity on the part of the founding generation to give sustained consideration to issues of religious freedom. For example, half a decade earlier, the controversy that had culminated in the adoption of Jefferson's Virginia Statute for Religious Freedom had generated extensive debate and scores of petitions signed by literally thousands of citizens. [23]

Against this backdrop of spirited discussion, the almost palpable apathy in Congress and the states regarding the Constitution's religion clauses may seem inexplicable.

But this apparent carelessness is instructive. If the enactors had conceived of their measure either as one that repudiated centuries of received wisdom or as one that ratified that wisdom in the face of emerging but determined and articulate opposition, it would indeed be anomalous that their discussions were so listless. Similarly, if the religion clauses had been understood as an effort to hammer out a compromise between these competing positions, we would expect that careful attention would have been given to the nature and terms of that compromise. Conversely, if the enactors believed that they were not answering the difficult questions at all but were merely deferring those questions to someone else—the states—then the complacent and lackluster character of the discussion is entirely understandable. But this conclusion also means that it is futile to seek in the framers' decision answers to substantive questions that the framers themselves chose not to address.

As against these arguments for an "essentially federalist" construction, however, proponents of a "side constraint" view may contend that the religion clauses cannot be viewed as a purely jurisdictional measure. [24] They may argue that the essential federalist view, with its denial of independent substantive content, rests on an assumption—that is, that the Constitution assigned *all* power over religion to the states—that is mistaken in at least two different senses. First, Congress retained power to regulate religion in areas subject to federal control, such as the territories and the District of Columbia. Second, and more generally, Congress had power to regulate religion under the necessary and proper clause. If the national government retained power to regulate religion, the argument would continue, then the limitations imposed on the national government by the religion clauses must have reflected more than a policy of federalism. They must have enacted, rather, a substantive right or principle of religious freedom applicable to the national government. The following discussion considers this objection more closely.

Religion and Territorial Powers

The argument that the religion clauses merely assigned authority over religion to the state governments may seem to founder on the fact that in federally controlled areas, such as the territories, there were no state governments to which such authority could be transferred; in those areas, at least, the national government *did* have power over religion.[25] Hence, it may be argued, if the religion clauses limited the national government in its powers of territorial governance, they must have done so by imposing substantive, as opposed to merely federalist or jurisdictional, limitations.

In the abstract, this argument seems plausible but hardly compelling. Assuming that Congress had power to regulate religion in the territories, we could, to be sure, treat the religion clauses as limiting that power by adopting some substantive right or principle of religious freedom. Conversely, we might argue that in its role as territorial governor, Congress acted essentially as a state and hence continued to enjoy all the powers that the religion clauses concededly left to the states (including, for example, the power to establish a state, or territorial, church). As a conceptual matter, either conclusion is possible. The important question, for present purposes, is not how this issue was ultimately resolved.[26] The immediate question, rather, is whether either of these conceptual possibilities reflected the meaning of the religion clauses as understood by those who proposed, discussed, and ratified them.

With respect to *that* question, however, the answer seems to be that the enactors of the religion clauses simply were not concerned with, and hence did not address, the question of Congress's power over religion in federally controlled areas. This omission is readily understandable when the religion clauses are viewed in their historical context. In the state conventions called to ratify the original Constitution, the Federalists had insisted that a bill of rights — and, more specifically, constitutional protection for religious freedom — was not needed, because Congress had no power to regulate religion in the first place.[27] Madison's statement in the Virginia convention expressed this view: "There is not a shadow of right in the general government to intermeddle with religion."[28] Opponents of the Constitution challenged these federalist denials of power, but *not* on the ground that Congress would have power to regulate religion in the territories. Their failure to press (or perhaps even think of) the territorial issue is not surprising. The anti-Federalists were worried about national power vis-à-vis *the states*; Congress's power to regulate religion in the territories was not their concern.

This same way of framing the issue naturally carried over into congressional discussion of the proposal that became the religion clauses.[29] In the House of Representatives, Roger Sherman of Connecticut reiterated the argument that no constitutional provision on the subject of religion was needed because Congress had no power to establish religion anyway. [30] Again, Sherman may have been wrong insofar as Congress did have power to regulate and establish religion in the territories. But no one challenged Sherman on this ground. Instead, Madison acknowledged that Sherman might be right but suggested that the provision would nonetheless help to allay fears expressed in the state conventions. [31]

In short, when proposing the religion clauses, Congress evidently was not concerned with, and hence paid no attention to, the subject of Congress's powers over religion in the territories. If this oversight seems odd, it is well to recall the apathy with which Congress treated the religion clauses, and indeed the Bill of Rights generally. The nation's representatives were loathe to consider the proposed Bill of Rights at all, believing that they had more important business to take care of. Despite his earlier opposition to the idea, Madison was obligated by a campaign promise to produce something in the nature of a bill of rights, but he was forced to coax and cajole—to "beg[ ] the House to indulge him"[32]—in order to persuade his colleagues even to consider his proposals.[33] Most of those who spoke on the issue opposed taking the time to consider a bill of rights; Madison's friend from Virginia, John Page, supported Madison's motion on the assumption that discussion of amendments would not "consume more than half an hour."[34]

The attitude with which Madison's proposals were received is reflected in a statement of Representative John Vining of Delaware. While grudgingly consenting (in view of "the anxiety [of] the honorable gentleman from Virginia") to postpone discussion of his own bill for establishing a land office, Vining commented regarding the land office bill that "in point of importance, every candid mind would acknowledge its preference."[35] In this complacent atmosphere, it is hardly surprising that the religion clauses might have been approved on the assumption that Congress had been denied power over religion—without congressional notice that this assumption was not entirely correct with respect to federally controlled areas, such as the territories.

Congress's subsequent behavior regarding areas within its control supports this interpretation. What is striking about that behavior is that in the early years of the Republic, Congress does not seem to have regarded itself as bound by any adopted constitutional principle controlling the relationship between government and religion. Consequently, congressional behavior in this period is an embarrassment both to the supporters of *Everson*'s "strict separation/no aid" construction and to the "nonpreferentialist" critics of *Everson*. Congress clearly *did* give material assistance to religion in the territories, especially in the provisions of Indian treaties and related laws.[36] Nonpreferentialists delight in recalling these instances of federal aid to religion when they rebut the "no aid" construction.[37] But if these instances undermine the contention that the establishment clause enacted a substantive "no aid" principle, they are likewise hard to square with the "nonpreferentialist" view, which holds that the establishment clause authorized government to aid religion only as long as such aid was equally available to all religions. In one treaty, for example, the national government specifically subsidized the Catholic Church; in another the aid was designated for the United Brethren.[38]

Such behavior is troubling as long as we assume that the religion clauses were understood by the founders as adopting some substantive principle regulating the relationship between government and religion. Conversely, if we relinquish that assumption, Congress's behavior becomes understandable. The religion clauses were understood as a federalist measure, not as the enactment of any substantive principle of religious freedom. Consequently, when later forced to deal with issues of religion in an area in which it *did* have jurisdiction, Congress acted in an ad hoc manner dictated by the particular circumstances; it did not seem to regard itself as being legally constrained by any substantive principle of religious freedom.

Religion and the "Necessary and Proper" Clause

An analogous objection to the jurisdictional construction of the religion clauses asserts that Congress possessed power to regulate religion under the "necessary and proper" clause of Article I, Section 8,[39] and hence that the restrictions placed on that power by the religion clauses must have been substantive in nature rather than merely jurisdictional. Unlike the objection based on federal power over religion in the territories, this argument cannot be dismissed on the ground that Congress did not consider the issue. In fact, opponents of the Constitution had made exactly this argument in the state ratifying conventions—that is, that despite Federalist disclaimers, Congress would in fact possess implied power over religion. The Federalists had denied this claim, but they could appreciate that this was a genuine concern, at least for some of the Anti-Federalists.[40] At the very least, as Douglas Laycock has pointed out, "the establishment clause was debated on the assumption that the government may have some power to aid religion. The Framers fought over how much of that hypothetical, unspecified, and possibly nonexistent power to restrain."[41]

By itself, however, the fact that the Federalists acknowledged possible federal implied power over religion does not entail the conclusion that the religion clauses adopted any substantive right or principle of religious freedom. On the contrary, the more natural inference is that the religion clauses were calculated simply to make explicit the jurisdictional division that both the Federalists and their opponents had professed to favor but that the Anti-Federalists thought was not clearly expressed in the Constitution itself. By this interpretation, the Federalists' position might have been described something as follows: "We believe, as we have consistently maintained, that explicit constitutional protection for religion is unnecessary, because the national government has no power to regulate or establish religion in the first place. You (the Anti-Federalists) fear that Congress *does* have such power, perhaps under the 'necessary and proper' clause. We disagree; but just in case you are right, and in order to demonstrate our good faith, we consent to make the lack of congressional power over religion explicit through a constitutional amendment."[42] By this view, the religion clauses served a clarifying and still jurisdictional purpose; they did not enact any substantive right or principle. Indeed, as Akhil Amar has pointed out, the very wording of the First Amendment suggests that it was understood as a sort of reverse "necessary and proper" clause.[43]

Although the framers *might* have amended the Constitution in this way, however, Gerard Bradley suggests that the text and background of the religion clauses do not support this interpretation. Bradley observes that one of the proposals discussed in the House of Representatives more aptly expressed the kind of complete denial of national jurisdiction over religion discussed above. At one point Representative Samuel Livermore of New Hampshire suggested that the amendment provide "that *Congress shall make no law touching religion*, or infringing the rights of conscience."[44] The final version of the religion clauses, of course, did not employ Livermore's language. Bradley infers that Congress believed itself to have substantive powers in matters of religion and rejected a proposal that would have eliminated those powers.[45]

Bradley's basic point is that, contrary to an argument advanced by Leonard Levy, one cannot plausibly transform an assumption that Congress lacks power over an area into a positive "no aid" principle restricting Congress even in areas in which Congress concededly *does* have power to legislate. Although Bradley's point is sound as far as it goes, his observations about the Livermore proposal do not support the view that the religion clauses were anything other than an assignment to the states of jurisdiction over matters of religion. In the first place, it is not clear that members of Congress understood the final version of the religion clauses to differ in any substantial way from the Livermore proposal. To be sure, changes in the wording of a proposed law often imply some dissatisfaction with the substance of versions not ultimately adopted. That inference can be mistaken, however, especially in a context in which legislators are apathetic or inattentive regarding a proposed measure. In that context, changes in a measure's language may not reflect deliberate alterations in substance so much as stylistic refinements or quirks or accidents in drafting. As noted above, the congressional atmosphere surrounding the proposed Bill of Rights was one of almost palpable indifference. Hence, arguments that place weight on proposals or drafts not finally adopted are tenuous, as debates among proponents and critics of a "nonpreferentialist" position already demonstrate. [46]

It is significant, moreover that Livermore's proposed language was initially adopted in the House of Representatives by a vote of 31 to 20. [47] When the various positions were reported back out of committee, Livermore's language had been modified, but recorded discussions do not reveal any explanation of this change; there is no recorded statement by a member of Congress indicating dissatisfaction with a purely jurisdictional measure and advocating a more substantive provision. In this context, the inference that Congress considered, initially accepted, and then later rejected a purely jurisdictional approach seems frail at best. [48]

More important, however, is that even if the abandonment of Livermore's language represented more than a stylistic adjustment or drafting accident, it hardly follows that Congress opted for a substantive right or principle rather than a jurisdictional and federalist position. After all, the language in Livermore's proposal that sounds most clearly jurisdictional — "Congress shall make no laws . . ." — was *not* abandoned but was instead retained in the final version of the religion clauses. The only difference is that the final version speaks of "no law," in the singular, rather than "no laws." What *did* change in the final version was the specification of what was included in this apparent renunciation of jurisdiction: The more sweeping phrase "touching religion" was ultimately replaced by a reference to laws "respecting an establishment of religion."[49] Bradley may be right that the final version is less inclusive than the Livermore language, but it hardly follows that Congress replaced a jurisdictional provision with a substantive right or principle. On the contrary, the natural conclusion is that Congress considered (in the Livermore proposal) a *general disclaimer of jurisdiction* over religion, but ultimately opted for a more limited or *partial disclaimer of jurisdiction* over religion.

Although the recorded debates do not reveal Congress's reasons for adopting this more cautious approach, it is not difficult to imagine why Congress might sensibly have come to favor a limited rather than a total renunciation of jurisdiction. Even though the religion question was regarded as one for the states rather than the national government to address, as the Federalists had argued all along, reflection might have made it clear that the national government would not be able to avoid matters of religion altogether. Such responsibility would arise not only in the governance of the territories, as discussed above, but also in an area that might have been more immediately conspicuous — that is, Congress's management of its own operations. For example, at the same time in which the Bill of Rights was being considered, both branches of Congress chose to appoint chaplains to begin each session with prayer.[50] Livermore's sweeping language — "no laws touching religion" — might have prohibited these actions. It is not implausible to suppose that a shift to a more limited renunciation of jurisdiction might have reflected a decision to retain power to adopt such measures.

In short, while wishing to leave the religion question with the states, where all sides had repeatedly insisted the question belonged, members of Congress may also have recognized that an absolute repudiation of national power to take *any* action "touching religion" was undesirable and probably impossible. Faced with this dilemma, one alternative might have been to confront the religion question directly, thrash out the large disagreements that divided the nation with respect to that question, and settle on a substantive answer to the religion question. It seems unlikely, however, that Congress could have reached consensus on any substantive answer to that question; and it is certain that Congress was not inclined to undertake such a Herculean labor.[51]

The other alternative was to opt for a partial renunciation of jurisdiction over religion. This solution would effectively assign to the states the major, controversial issues of religion—issues regarding the "establishment" and regulation of religion—and it would defer the residual, nonassignable issues of religion to the future. In this way, Congress would be spared the likely impossible task of trying to debate and agree on the proper relationship between government and religion, and would thus be enabled to get on with the business that most members regarded as more deserving of congressional attention (such as providing for land offices).

The historical evidence is too sparse to permit a definitive conclusion in favor of this specific aspect of the original understanding. What we *can* say is that in the historical context such a course might have seemed sensible and attractive and that if Congress *had* made a decision in favor of a partial disclaimer of jurisdiction, the religion clauses as adopted would have been a suitable way of expressing that decision. In addition, Congress's contemporaneous decisions, for example, to appoint chaplains and authorize Thanksgiving proclamations, suggest that Congress did not believe itself to be bound by a substantive principle of religious freedom that would have constrained its authority in these matters.

The possible flaw in this interpretation is that, like most modern interpretations of the religion clauses, it may simply attribute to the enactors greater attention and thought than they actually gave to those clauses. This objection to the "partial disclaimer" construction, however, only serves to reinforce the more general thesis of this chapter: Given the serious differences in opinion that existed with regard to the religion question, and in view of the largely indifferent attitude taken by Congress and the states to the religion clauses, it is implausible to view those clauses as expressing a decision in favor of any substantive answer to a difficult and controversial question. Congress could avoid answering that troublesome question by simply deferring it—to the states primarily, and in part, perhaps, to the future. Not surprisingly, that is just what Congress chose to do.

3

Is the Free Exercise
Clause Different?

In the previous chapter I referred to "the religion clauses" as if they constituted a unitary provision. This undifferentiated treatment may seem to overlook a critical distinction. It is conceivable, after all, that the establishment clause was a purely jurisdictional measure but that the free exercise clause was more than that. Arguing in this vein, some scholars have acknowledged the difficulty of extending the establishment clause to the states through "incorporation" into the Fourteenth Amendment, but have argued that the free exercise clause *does* contain independent substantive content that can support constitutional restrictions applicable to the national and state governments.[1]

Akhil Amar has recently contended for this view. While conceding that the establishment clause was a federalist measure that cannot without distortion be extended to the states, Amar reaches just the opposite conclusion with respect to the free exercise clause:

> [T]he free exercise clause was paradigmatically about citizen rights, not state rights; it thus invites incorporation. Indeed, this clause was specially concerned with the plight of minority religions, and thus meshes especially well with the minority-rights thrust of the Fourteenth Amendment. Yet unlike incorporation of the establishment clause, application of free exercise principles does not wholly negate states' rights under the original establishment clause. A state would be free to establish one or several churches, but would be obliged to respect the free exercise rights

of dissenters to opt out. Official establishment is of course not necessarily incompatible with freedom of worship and religious toleration, as England today attests. The American experience confirms this. Although Massachusetts had state-supported churches until 1833, her constitution of 1780 explicitly guaranteed freedom of conscience for religious dissenters — in a provision that immediately preceded language authorizing government-supported churches. [2]

Conflict Between the Clauses?

The position urged by scholars like Amar necessarily assumes a significant difference in the content and purposes of the establishment and free exercise clauses. In the modern context, that assumption seems natural enough. Judges and scholars have devoted considerable analysis, after all, to explaining how the establishment clause differs from the free exercise clause. This analysis has often depicted the clauses as not merely independent in content but as *opposed* in their basic purposes: The establishment clause has been understood as *prohibiting* (at least in some circumstances) governmental support for or accommodation of religion, [3] while the free exercise clause has been understood as *requiring* (at least in some circumstances) governmental accommodation of religion. Extensive analysis has been dedicated to resolving, or at least reducing, this perceived conflict between the clauses. [4]

It appears, however, that the whole notion of a conflict or even a disjunction between the religion clauses is of modern origins. In the founding period, "establishment" and "free exercise" were not viewed as distinct concerns. John Noonan notes that "[f]or Madison, there was no substantial difference between outright persecution and establishment of a religion." [5] Not surprisingly, therefore, nothing in the recorded discussions in Congress suggests that the legislators regarded the clauses as serving conflicting, or even distinct, purposes. [6] T. Jeremy Gunn observes that "[i]f Roger Sherman intended to say what he is recorded as having said, the implication is that the two clauses (no establishment and no infringement of rights of conscience) were seen to constitute but one principle in his mind." [7] More generally, Thomas Curry asserts:

[T]o see the two clauses as separate, balanced, competing, or carefully worked out prohibitions designed to meet different eventualities would be to read into the minds of the actors far more than was there. . . . Contemporaries did not, for example, distinguish between religious oppression as falling under the ban of the "free exercise" clause and a general assessment as being prohibited by the "establishment" clause. As the debates in Virginia in the mid-1780s had shown, the opponents of tax support of religion fought it primarily as a violation of the state's free exercise guarantee and only incidentally as an establishment. Isaac Backus and the Baptists pursued the same path in New England. . . . Similarly, those who espoused government support defended it primarily as fair, equitable, and compatible with religious freedom and concerned themselves very little with the issue of establishment.[8]

Recognizing the unitary quality of the provision, Mary Ann Glendon and Raul Yanes have recently suggested that we should refer to the religion *clause*, in the singular, rather than to the religion clauses.[9] Other commentators take a similar view.[10] If these commentators are correct,[11] however, then it is untenable to assert that the establishment clause was a purely jurisdictional measure but that the free exercise clause created an independent substantive right or principle of religious freedom.

Free Exercise Controversies in the Founding Period

This unitary construction of the religion clauses is reinforced by the fact that the same arguments that support a jurisdictional construction of the establishment clause apply to the free exercise clause as well. As discussed in the previous chapter, the traditional and voluntarist positions on the religion question agreed that religion was essential to a stable social order; they disagreed over the efficacy of governmental support for religion. Such support, if appropriate, might take the form of monetary aid to religion, but it might also consist of governmental enforcement of a religious regimen or of legal sanctions against deviant or unorthodox beliefs and practices. In other words, the opposition between the traditional and voluntarist positions affected both the "establishment" and "free exercise" aspects of the issue, and the same divisions that prevented Congress from agreeing on any substantive solution to "establishment" or "aid" issues would thus have precluded the adoption of a substantive principle of "free exercise" as well.

In fact states did provide, in differing and often controversial ways, nonmonetary support to or enforcement of the dominant religion. Such support commonly included religious tests for public office, Sabbath-observance laws, and prohibitions against blasphemy. A brief overview of such laws suggests the divided state of opinion during the founding period regarding what today would be called "free exercise" issues — and, consequently, the difficulty of reconciling such differences in any generally acceptable principle of religious freedom.

Throughout the founding period, most states maintained religious requirements for public office. These requirements differed from state to state; the category of citizens excluded from office might include non-Protestants, or non-Christians, or non-Trinitarians, or persons who did not believe in a deity and an afterlife. [12] Such exclusions provoked extensive debate; consequently, some states altered while others retained these exclusions during the founding period. [13]

Similarly, some states had laws prohibiting blasphemy. For example, in relatively liberal Pennsylvania it was a crime to "wilfully, premeditatively, and despitefully blaspheme, or speak lightly or profanely of Almighty God, Christ Jesus, the Holy Spirit, or the Scriptures of Truth." [14] Well into the nineteenth century, these laws continued to be enforced. [15] They were, however, a source of controversy; [16] not only the defendants in blasphemy prosecutions but also statesmen such as Jefferson and John Adams regarded blasphemy laws as a violation of religious freedom. [17] Other prominent figures, such as Joseph Story and Chancellor Kent, took a contrary view; indeed, Kent found that blasphemy was a common-law crime and approved a blasphemy prosecution even though New York had no statutory prohibition. [18]

Most states also enacted laws requiring Sabbath observance, but these laws differed significantly in content. Virginia's Sabbath law (proposed, incidentally, by James Madison on the same day on which he introduced the Virginia Bill for Religious Freedom [19]) was relatively mild; it merely prohibited unnecessary labor and disruption of worship services. [20] By contrast, New England states prohibited "unnecessary walking" and imposed fines for irregular attendance at church services. [21]

These divergent views suggest that just as it would have been impossible for the founders to reach any consensus on the issue of "establishment," they likewise could not have achieved any general agreement on the issue of "free exercise"[22] (even if they had viewed this as an independent issue, as they likely did not). Once again, the natural course for the First Congress was not to attempt any substantive answer to such questions but rather to leave such controversies to the states, where the Constitution's supporters had all along insisted that matters of religion belonged anyway.

As with the establishment clause, moreover, the lack of substantive discussion regarding the free exercise clause in Congress or in the ratifying legislatures suggests that this is just what the clause was understood as doing. Indeed, this inference is even stronger with respect to the free exercise clause than it is for the establishment clause. If those clauses are treated as independent, then virtually all the reported congressional discussion concerned what came to be the establishment clause;[23] there was virtually no discussion at all of what we now call the free exercise clause.[24] Once again, this apparent apathy contrasts strikingly with the energy with which free exercise issues could be debated when citizens attempted to codify a free exercise right at the *state* level.[25] Given this record, it is wholly implausible to suppose that the enactors of the free exercise clause attempted to formulate any substantive principle or right that might be the basis for answering the divisive questions that modern judges and scholars would place under the heading of "free exercise."

A Free Exercise Consensus?

While recognizing that the division in opinion within the country militated against the possibility of a substantive national policy on the subject of "establishment," Michael McConnell suggests that consensus prevailed regarding the issue of free exercise, thus permitting enactment of a substantive right of religious freedom.[26] On the face of things, this suggestion seems inconsistent with the pattern of laws limiting office-holding on religious grounds, punishing blasphemy, and requiring Sabbath observance. That pattern might suggest that if there was a consensus at all, it was *opposed* to the "free exercise of religion" in anything like the contemporary sense of that term.[27] Once it is recognized that both the meaning and the desirability of these laws enforcing religion were controversial, however, the more realistic assessment is that free exercise issues, like establishment issues, were the source of significant disagreement in the founding period.

The assertion of a consensus is based largely on the fact that most state constitutions of the period contained "free exercise" or "freedom of conscience" provisions.[28] To conclude from this, however, that consensus prevailed (even "in principle") is to ignore the deep divisions that existed regarding what "freedom of conscience" meant.[29] Terms commonly used in discussing this issue are likely to mislead contemporary students, thereby generating anachronistic conclusions. For example, Americans of the late eighteenth century commonly distinguished between "freedom" and "license," or the abuse of freedom,[30] and "licentiousness" was a capacious category that might include any immorality or breach of civil law.[31] Consistent with this usage, Americans of the time could easily endorse "freedom of conscience" but also dismiss a claim offered under that heading as mere "licentiousness."[32] Or, consistent with precedent going back at least as far as Augustine[33] and perhaps the New Testament[34] (or, if an American and Protestant authority is wanted, John Cotton),[35] opponents of particular beliefs or behavior could readily characterize such beliefs or behavior not as the product of conscience but rather as a form of "sinning *against* conscience." In addition, Bernard Bailyn notes that John Adams, in defending Massachusetts' laws establishing religion, argued that these were based on the consciences of Massachusetts citizens, "and therefore 'the very liberty of conscience' sought by the Baptists demanded, by extension, that the laws in question be retained."[36]

Virtually all Americans of the time also agreed that freedom of conscience or of religion did not include any right to disturb the public peace,[37] and state constitutions sometimes made this limitation explicit.[38] The qualifier had an elastic quality. For example, punishment of blasphemy was not an infringement of religious freedom, the orthodox maintained, because blasphemy disturbed the public peace by upsetting majoritarian religious sensibilities.[39]

In short, while Americans may have concurred in endorsing the slogan "freedom of conscience," the agreement was largely verbal. There clearly was *not* agreement about the substantive content or meaning to be given to that slogan.[40] To be sure, advocates of opposing views may have competed to invoke the appealing rhetoric of "freedom of conscience." But to conclude from this practice that consensus prevailed or even that the various antagonists agreed "in principle" would be like concluding that proponents and opponents of abortion rights, or proponents and opponents of school voucher programs, are actually in essential agreement because they all attempt to deploy the rhetoric of "choice."[41]

Freedom of Religion in the Northwest Ordinance

A possible challenge to this construction arises from the Northwest Ordinance, adopted by the Congress under the Articles of Confederation in 1787 and reenacted by the new Congress in 1789. Article 1 of the ordinance provided that in the Northwest Territory "[n]o person demeaning himself in a peaceable and orderly manner shall ever be molested on account of his mode of worship or religious sentiments."[42] This language appears to be a free exercise provision that adopted a substantive right or principle. And if Congress was capable of adopting a substantive right of religious freedom for a territory, might it not have done the same for the nation as a whole — subject, of course, to a federalist side constraint?

This inference seems dubious, however, for at least two reasons. First, it is significant that, as one historian has observed, "[a]fter a careful comparison of the phraseology of the corresponding clauses in the constitutions of the different States, all evidence points toward . . . the Massachusetts Constitution" as the source of the Northwest Ordinance provision.[43] The Massachusetts Constitution was understood to permit state subsidization of religion, religious qualifications for public office, blasphemy prosecutions, and stringent Sabbath laws. It is hardly surprising, therefore, that a comparable provision might seem acceptable even to states that rejected the idea of religious freedom in anything like either a Jeffersonian or a more contemporary sense.

More important is that even if article 1 of the Northwest Ordinance is viewed as creating an important substantive right to religious freedom for the territory, we could not infer that a similar right or principle either was or could have been adopted for the nation as a whole. It is instructive to note that the Northwest Ordinance also prohibited slavery and involuntary servitude, and yet "the southern majority then in Congress . . . readily accepted" this provision.[44] If this southern acquiescence seems surprising, we must remember that Congress was anxious to encourage settlement of the territory both because Congress wished to secure the territory against British and Spanish influences and because the sale of territorial lands was expected to be a major source of desperately needed revenue.[45] If a prohibition on slavery would encourage settlement, southern states were quite willing to go along; they assumed that the provision implied no condemnation of slavery elsewhere.[46]

In the same way, religious intolerance would naturally discourage migration to an area by anyone adhering to an unpreferred faith, as Madison's "Memorial and Remonstrance" had recently pointed out.[47] Hence, it is not surprising that a Congress anxious to promote migration would favor religious tolerance or freedom for the area.

In reality, it is hard to imagine that any denomination could have achieved dominance in the Northwest Territory in any event. By the late 1780s, a variety of denominations, including Anglicans, Presbyterians, and Methodists, had been evangelizing in the territory, while the religious faith in this country perhaps most disposed to publicly supported religion—the New England Congregationalists—was relatively slow to arrive.[48] When the Congregationalists later became more active in the area, the pluralistic situation "brought them to accept the facts of political and religious heterogeneity," thereby changing Congregationalist attitudes toward church-state relations.[49] In this respect, the Northwest Territory reflects the American experience generally, in which a commitment to broader religious freedom has evolved of necessity out of the fact of religious pluralism.[50] By approving the Northwest Ordinance in 1787 and 1789, however, Congress was not expressing an existing consensus favoring a substantive principle of religious freedom in general any more than it was expressing a consensus favoring the prohibition of slavery in general.

The Jurisdictional Free Exercise Clause

Given the controversies that in fact existed in the new nation over "free exercise" issues, it seems most plausible to understand the free exercise clause, like the establishment clause, as expressing a jurisdictional decision to leave the substantive issues to be resolved by the states. Thomas Curry cogently expresses the point:

> [A]ll Americans could accept "phraseology" protecting the "rights of conscience" or banning the imposition of "articles of faith" or the "establishment of one sect in preference to another." They disagreed, however, over the substantive meaning of such terms. A majority of Virginians, for example, had clearly demonstrated that in their view a general assessment violated the "rights of

conscience," while a majority of the inhabitants of Massachusetts obviously felt it did not. Both states proclaimed equal devotion to the term "rights of conscience," but because all believed that such matters pertained to the states, and that they were making explicit the fact that the federal government had nothing to do with religion, no collision of their differing views as to what constituted a violation of "rights of conscience" took place.[51]

Nothing in the text of the free exercise clause contradicts this conclusion. Some scholars have suggested that the language of the free exercise clause sounds like it is recognizing a substantive right.[52] Although the clause did not use the term *right*, it is true that the clause imposed substantive limitations on the power of Congress. But that observation proves nothing. As discussed in the previous chapter, even a purely jurisdictional measure will necessarily impose substantive restrictions on one level of government to ensure that the substantive area is left to a different level of government. Thus, the presence of substantive language in no way qualifies or negates the federalist character of a provision such as the free exercise clause.

On the contrary, such a substantive limitation would seem to be a necessary part of an essentially federalist position. It would be futile to say that religion was within the states' sole jurisdiction if the national government were not thereby forbidden to regulate or prohibit the exercise of religions it might not favor. Hence, something like the free exercise clause would have to be stated or implied in order to effect an essentially federalist solution to the religion question.

4

The Nullification of
Original Meaning

Modern legal scholarship considering the historical meaning of the religion clauses presents a spectacle of frustration. Some of that scholarship is sloppy and tendentious — "law office" history [1] — while some is searching and careful. But even the most careful efforts seem to have brought us no closer to any consensus or any demonstrably correct construction regarding the religion clauses. The foregoing discussion suggests that this failure was foreordained in the questions that modern judges and scholars have asked. In addition, the misconceived focus of the modern inquiry means that even when scholars admit defeat in the originalist quest, they do so for the wrong reasons, and they mistake the consequences of giving up on original meaning.

Asking the Wrong Question

Originalist scholarship in this area has been driven by a question that for judges and legal scholars seems both natural and important: What sort of principle — or what right or theory — of religious freedom did the religion clauses adopt? This question has immediately led lawyers to confront a serious obstacle — the apparent scarcity of direct evidence. As noted earlier, the enactors of the religion clauses just didn't say much about the substantive meaning or scope of the principle of religious freedom that they were, supposedly, writing into the nation's fundamental law.

Faced with this difficulty, judges and legal scholars have done what they could with the meager direct evidence available. They have, for instance, valiantly wrung meanings out of the word *respecting* (in "no law *respecting* an establishment of religion"),[2] and they have argued over the significance of the framers' use of the indefinite rather than the definite article ("*an* establishment of religion").[3] By and large, however, the paucity of direct evidence has forced judges and scholars to resort to indirect evidence in a two-step interpretive process. The first step has been to identify evidence of what one or more of the framers or their contemporaries said or thought, not necessarily about *the religion clauses* per se, but about *the subject of religious freedom*. The second step has been to superimpose this opinion or view about *religious freedom* onto the *religion clauses*.

At the first stage of this process, judges and scholars have found ample material to work on. The enactors of the religion clauses may not have said much of substance in debating those clauses, but in other contexts many of them and their contemporaries expressed themselves voluminously on issues of religious freedom. Hence, judges and scholars have found a wealth of indirect evidence from which to fashion an interpretation — or, rather, a multitude of conflicting interpretations.

The difficulty has arisen at the second stage, when the judge or scholar attempts to impose a particular historical view of religious freedom onto the religion clauses. This attribution inevitably generates an obvious question: Assuming that we can reconstruct Jefferson's, or Madison's, or the Commonwealth of Virginia's views about religious freedom (often a perilous task in its own right), what is the justification for ascribing those views to the framers or ratifiers of the religion clauses as a body?

Some expositions simply ignore this problem. For example, the majority opinion in *Everson v. Board of Education* described the content of Jefferson's Virginia Statute for Religious Freedom and then confidently asserted that the establishment clause had the same meaning.[4] Remarkably, the Court took no notice of the obvious objections to imposing the Virginia policy on a constitutional provision that had an entirely different wording and that was adopted by a different, and very differently composed, body.[5]

Other, more responsible scholarship worries about such difficulties[6] — but without successfully resolving them. Indeed, scholars may come to despair of the possibility that we will ever be able to determine which eighteenth-century view of religious freedom the framers intended to adopt. [7] It seems that the very obstacle that makes resort to the two-step interpretive procedure necessary in the first place—that is, the apparent scarcity of direct evidence of the original understanding—also makes that procedure powerless to show that a view of religious freedom held by any particular person or group was adopted generally by the framers and ratifiers of the religion clauses. Thus, Donald Drakeman, criticizing "judges, lawyers, scholars, and many others [who] continue to try to cram volumes of meaning into ten words virtually devoid of clear intent on the historical record before us," observes that "suggestions about how to interpret the establishment clause based on the framers' intentions are just short of complete speculation because they are based solely on the extremely sparse and highly questionable historical records. The records simply contain too little evidence." [8] "[M]odern commentators," Drakeman asserts, "have made a constitutional mountain out of a congressional molehill." [9]

The foregoing analysis shows how this diagnosis, for all of its apparent plausibility, is nonetheless misconceived. It is true, as Drakeman suggests, that modern commentators typically make "a Constitutional mountain out of a congressional molehill" and that contemporary constructions of the religion clauses typically are supported by "extremely sparse and highly questionable" evidence. Drakeman attributes these failures to a supposed paucity of historical evidence. In other words, the framers' intentions *would be* relevant if we could recover those intentions; the problem is that because the historical record is so sketchy, our suppositions about original meaning are inevitably speculative.

The argument of this book suggests, on the contrary, that the evidence is not sparse; the problem, rather, is that contemporary scholars and judges, of both the "separationist" and "accommodationist" varieties, have doggedly refused to acknowledge its import. The evidence is more than sufficient to show, with as much certainty as is to be expected in these matters, that the religion clauses did no more and no less than confirm the constitutional allocation of jurisdiction over religion to the states. Although clear enough, however, that construction is also disappointing because it rudely refuses to satisfy the judges' and scholars' hunger for a substantive right or principle of religious freedom. In short, the original meaning is not relevant in principle but unknowable in practice, as scholars like

Drakeman suppose; it is, rather, knowable but unresponsive to present demands.

Legal scholars sometimes actually state this conclusion without seeming to recognize that they have in fact described the original meaning that they purport to be searching for. As noted, for example, Donald Drakeman pronounces the original meaning irrecoverable. But in another section of his book, he confidently asserts that "[i]f someone had been prescient enough to think of [modern church-state problems], the Founding Fathers would almost assuredly have said: 'That's none of our business. We're here to put shackles on this new federal Congress, not to decide some local tax or schooling issues.'"[10] Drakeman further observes that "members of the First Congress were ducking all important (that is, state and local) church-state issues. Church-state controversies were abundant before and after 1789, but they did not surface in the United States Congress because they were not federal issues."[11] Since the evidence is apparently more than ample to support *these* observations about the framers' intent, why does Drakeman also insist that the evidence is sparse and that conclusions about original meaning are "just short of complete speculation"?

The answer, it seems, is that this jurisdictional meaning is simply not the kind of original meaning that Drakeman, and other contemporary scholars and judges, are looking for. As discussed earlier in this chapter, these scholars start with a basic question: What principle, or what right or theory, of religious freedom did the religion clauses adopt? *That* question assumes in advance that the religion clauses were designed to provide a substantive answer to the religion question — that they were designed to prescribe, in at least a skeletal way, the proper relationship between government and religion. The modern problem is to figure out what that prescription was. Hence, evidence of *other* intentions is duly noted and then promptly set aside, because the other intentions — more precisely, the jurisdictional intentions — are unresponsive to the questions scholars are asking.

But if the framers were not addressing the modern scholars' questions, then this common approach simply ensures that scholars will not be able to see the original meaning even when it is, so to speak, staring them in the face. As long as legal scholarship continues to insist that the historical evidence answer a question that was in fact deferred, in short, such scholarship will be doomed to continuing frustration and disappointment. The solution to this difficulty lies in recognizing that the question itself is misconceived.

The Repeal of the Religion Clauses

Scholars have sometimes argued that historical evidence does not support the position that the framers of the Fourteenth Amendment intended to incorporate the religion clauses and thus make them applicable to the states. In addition, some scholars have pointed out that the "incorporation" of the establishment clause, because of its federalist character, is conceptually awkward. [12] The foregoing discussion suggests that these observations, although correct as far as they go, understate both the difficulties and the significance of the "incorporation" of the religion clauses.

As argued above, the religion clauses amounted to a decision by the national government not to address substantive questions concerning the proper relationship between religion and government. There would be no *national* law, theory, or principle—and, consequently, no *constitutional* law, theory, or principle—prescribing the proper relationship between religion and government. The decision to "incorporate" the religion clauses represented, in effect, the reversal of that decision. By undertaking to review and regulate church-state relations at both the national and state levels, the federal judiciary necessarily committed itself to developing a substantive constitutional law for the subject. It would therefore be more accurate to say that this decision, far from "incorporating" the religion clauses, effectively repudiated—and hence repealed—those clauses. [13]

To put the matter in slightly different terms: The framers managed to avoid addressing the first-order or substantive question of religious freedom by answering the second-order, jurisdictional question in a particular way. The 1940s Supreme Court rejected the framers' answer to the jurisdictional question; consequently, the Court was required to—and *did*—undertake to answer the substantive question. On both counts, therefore, the Court took a position just opposite that reflected in the original religion clauses.

This conclusion underscores the futility of trying to derive or develop an account of religious freedom for contemporary use from the original religion clauses. The earlier discussion suggested that those clauses did not address substantive questions of religious freedom. It now appears, in addition, that the original decision embodied in the religion clauses was effectively repealed by their so-called incorporation into the Fourteenth Amendment.

As a matter of logic, at least, this effective repeal has far-reaching but thus far unappreciated consequences. For example, even scholars who have criticized the incorporation of the establishment clause have typically assumed that the clause continues to restrict the national government, as it was originally intended to do.[14] But even that assumption seems unwarranted. If the religion clauses were an allocation of jurisdiction over religion to the states, and if that allocation has now been undone, then there is no justification—no *originalist* justification grounded in the First Amendment's religion clauses, at least—for holding even the national government to restrictions grounded in a jurisdictional arrangement that has long since been repudiated.

More generally, the effort to develop an authoritative constitutional law of religious freedom based on the religion clauses of the First Amendment is in a sense similar to an effort to discuss the states' current constitutional authority to permit or regulate liquor on the basis of the Eighteenth Amendment, while ignoring the inconvenient fact that this amendment has been repealed. If there is to be constitutional law on either subject, it will have to be derived from some other source.

Postscript: New Claims for the Fourteenth Amendment

The general debate about whether the Fourteenth Amendment incorporated the Bill of Rights is, of course, an old one—and one not likely to die away soon. The preceding discussion has not directly addressed that general debate, because if the religion clauses as originally understood were purely jurisdictional, as I have argued, then they contained no substantive right or principle of religious freedom that could have been "incorporated" even if the enactors of the Fourteenth Amendment had wanted to incorporate them. However, as I was working on final revisions of this book, Professor Kurt Lash kindly sent me the draft of an article advancing claims that, if correct, would present this issue in a new light.[15]

Lash appears to agree that the establishment clause, as originally understood, was a purely federalist measure, and he understands the free exercise clause to have had very limited substantive content. However, Lash argues that in ensuing decades Americans came to *believe* (albeit incorrectly, at least from an originalist perspective) that those clauses had greater substantive content and scope than their framers had intended. Consequently, the enactors of the Fourteenth Amendment incorporated the religion clauses, but not in their original meaning; rather they incorporated the religion clauses *as those clauses had come to be understood*. Thus, Lash suggests that "[i]f, by the time of the adoption of the Fourteenth Amendment, the Establishment Clause was regarded as expressing individual rights the federalism argument loses its sting."[16] Similarly, he alludes to the "second adoption" of the free exercise clause.

Lash is almost surely correct in asserting that understandings of the religion clauses changed over time. Clearly the Supreme Court's understanding of the religion clauses had changed dramatically by the 1940s, and there is no reason to doubt that this process of changing (and conflicting) constructions began virtually as soon as the First Amendment was adopted. It seems likely, for example, that Madison's views about constitutional religious freedom changed noticeably during his lifetime. Thus, it is entirely plausible, as Lash argues, that by the 1860s, when the Fourteenth Amendment was drafted and enacted, at least some citizens and legislators believed the religion clauses to have greater substantive content and scope than the framers of 1789 had intended them to have.

This observation might deflect — albeit with some perhaps unexpected consequences, to be discussed shortly — one kind of objection to the standard "incorporation" position. It might deflect, that is, the objection developed here that the Fourteenth Amendment *could not* have incorporated the religion clauses because those clauses contained no substantive principle or right to incorporate. I say "might" because Lash's thesis also raises a conceptual question about how to characterize the "incorporation" decision attributed to the Fourteenth Amendment's enactors. Did the enactors intend to incorporate their own (mistaken) understanding of the religion clauses? Lash describes the situation in this way, but there is another possible description: The enactors of the Fourteenth Amendment might have intended to incorporate the original meaning of the religion clauses, *whatever that original meaning was*. To be sure, they had opinions about the original meaning of those clauses, but what they intended to incorporate, perhaps, was the "real" original meaning, not their opinions about that meaning. If this latter characterization is adopted, Lash's claims are still interesting historically, but they do nothing to defeat or avoid the objection developed above.

It is difficult to know how to choose between these characterizations from within an originalist framework. We can hardly ask which characterization more accurately captures the Fourteenth Amendment enactors' intentions; the enactors presumably did not believe that their opinions about the original meaning were mistaken and hence would not have consciously confronted the alternatives that Lash's claims raise. Assuming the enactors held originalist assumptions, in other words, it is unlikely that they would have asked themselves: "Are we incorporating the actual original meaning of the religion clauses, or are we incorporating our mistaken understanding of that meaning?" One might try to deal with the problem through "imaginative reconstruction": [17] If the enactors *had* considered this choice, which alternative *would* they have preferred? But the answer to this counterfactual question is not obvious. One might argue that what the enactors were trying to do was to put their own notions of religious freedom into the Constitution; surely, therefore, they would have wanted to incorporate their own understanding of the religion clauses, even if that understanding was incorrect as a reading of history. But perhaps the enactors of the Fourteenth Amendment disagreed in their own ideas about religious freedom, just as Americans disagreed in the founding era—and as they still do today. It is commonplace that in such situations of disagreement, legislators sometimes defer, or "delegate," the substantive decision. So in this case, the enactors might have "delegated backward" by incorporating whatever principle of religious freedom the original framers had adopted.

Since the inquiry concerns an imaginary or hypothetical decision anyway, it is difficult to know how to choose between these "reconstructions." Suppose, though, that we choose Lash's characterization. If so, then we avoid one kind of objection to incorporation, but the argument must still confront the more familiar historical objection, which asserts that the enactors of the Fourteenth Amendment simply did not intend to incorporate the Bill of Rights, or at least the religion clauses, at all. As noted above, the incorporation debate is a long-standing one; William Nelson observes that "[v]oluminous evidence has been presented in support of both the expansive and the narrow readings of the Fourteenth Amendment's history."[18] This book is not the place to rehearse that debate. It is important to recall, though, that the case for incorporation of the religion clauses raises a special issue because of the Blaine Amendment, which Congress considered in 1875 and 1876.

The Blaine Amendment, as Daniel Conkle points out, contained the exact language of the First Amendment's religion clauses except that it applied to the states, not to Congress. Hence, the Blaine Amendment would have done precisely what, according to the incorporation argument, the Fourteenth Amendment had already done several years earlier. The proposal was debated at some length; it passed in the House but was defeated in the Senate. [19] The critical fact, Conkle argues, is that although many of the legislators who had drafted and debated the Fourteenth Amendment were still in Congress, "[t]he record is replete with evidence that the Blaine Amendment's application of the religion clauses to the states was not thought superfluous by either the supporters or the opponents of the proposed enactment." [20]

Lash attempts to overcome the argument against incorporation. Although his evidence on this issue does not in my view appreciably strengthen the case for incorporation, his claims deserve close attention. What is most important for purposes of this book, however, is that if Lash's claims are convincing, they call for a major reorientation in constitutional discourse about religious freedom. From *Everson* on, the extensive historical efforts in this field have focused on the colonial and founding periods; the critical evidence has included Jefferson's Virginia Statute for Religious Freedom, Madison's "Memorial and Remonstrance," and the discussions in the First Congress. If Lash is right, all these sources recede in relevance; Madison and Jefferson, Isaac Backus and John Leland, would be displaced as definers of constitutional religious freedom by John Bingham, Thaddeus Stevens, Charles Sumner, and their contemporaries. Originalist scholars and judges would look to discern the views about the relationship between government and religion that prevailed, not in the founding period, but rather in the post-Civil War reconstruction era.

It would be a mistake to suppose that this reorientation would easily permit constitutional law in this field to carry on with business as usual, with only a change in the historical authorities listed in the footnotes. On the contrary, it seems likely that prevalent notions about the relationship between government and religion had changed significantly between 1790 and 1865 — and not necessarily in a liberal or secular direction. Henry May notes that the Virginia Statute for Religious Freedom was enacted during a brief historical moment — he calls it "the Jeffersonian moment" — when the forces of the revolutionary enlightenment and of evangelical Protestantism happened to converge. [21] This convergence soon disappeared, however, as the Jeffersonian moment was swept away by, among other things, the powerful currents of religious revivalism. [22] Continuing this story, Jon Butler describes the nineteenth century as the scene of a sustained campaign of Christianization. [23] Butler observes that "[a]s Christianization advanced in America, new and sometimes ugly demands for government guarantees of Christian hegemony emerged rather than receded."[24] In fact, Butler argues, the "Christian nation" conception of the Republic, with an accompanying construction of the founding and of the First Amendment, developed and took hold in the mid-nineteenth century, not earlier.[25]

Lash himself asserts that as the nineteenth century progressed, the Jeffersonian notion of "separation" between church and state receded in favor of greater religious activism in public affairs and of what Lash calls "Religious Republicanism"—that is, the view that government should promote religion in the interest of the community.[26] Although Lash plainly does not propose to read these notions into constitutional law, his observations underscore a crucial point: If a new originalism is to be based on a revisionist account of the Fourteenth Amendment, the picture of government's relation to religion that this new originalism produces will likely look very different than anything that would have recommended itself either to Thomas Jefferson or to the justices in *Everson*.

5

The Theory Project

We cannot determine which among the numerous principles of religious freedom is "the Constitution's principle" by looking to the original meaning of the religion clauses. But if originalism cannot tell us what religious freedom means under the Constitution, what alternative is left us? To many legal scholars, the answer may seem evident: If text and history cannot determine what religious freedom means under the Constitution, then we must undertake a theoretical assessment of the various versions of religious freedom to determine which of those versions is the most plausible, or the most theoretically attractive. [1]

Much modern legal scholarship is devoted to just this task—that is, articulating a theoretical defense and elaboration of one or another principle prescribing the appropriate relationship between government and religion. The next several chapters assess that theoretical enterprise. Before considering specific theoretical approaches and problems, however, it is helpful to reflect briefly on the nature of this project. What is it that prompts lawyers and judges to seek refuge in "theory"? What do they hope to achieve, and are those hopes realistic? Is theorizing inevitable, or are there alternatives?

The Theoretical Imperative

The attractiveness of theory to legal scholars is not new. Harold Berman has observed that in the West (but not necessarily in other periods and cultures), lawyers and scholars have for centuries thought of law as "a coherent whole, an integrated system, a 'body.'"[2] Similarly, many scholars have wanted law to be a "science."[3] This determination to see law as a coherent whole or as a science naturally nurtures the theory-building inclinations of legal scholars.

In this century, however, and especially in the last few decades, the theoretical impulse has manifested itself in distinctive ways. The modern project can be understood against the backdrop of Legal Realism. In the 1920s and 1930s the Realists showed that the materials of traditional law — that is, judicial precedents, enacted statutes and constitutional provisions, and conventional techniques for analyzing these authorities — were more chaotic than had been supposed.[4] The Realist challenge threatened the image of law as a coherent whole or as a science and thus forced legal scholars to look for new ways of imposing order on the law. Not surprisingly, scholars eventually turned to "theory" — primarily to economic theory and, especially in constitutional law, to political and moral philosophy.

Perhaps the most conspicuous exemplar of this theoretical turn has been Bruce Ackerman. In an early essay, Ackerman applauded the Legal Realists' critical achievement but, noting that the legacy of Realism had been merely an intense concern with legal process, lamented their "failure to develop a coherent social philosophy" and their "refusal to assess decisions in terms of a substantive theory about the good society."[5] In later works, Ackerman set out to remedy this deficiency. In *Private Property and the Constitution*,[6] he looked at "takings" cases and, in a Realist spirit, found them to be hopelessly confused. He concluded that traditional legal techniques were inadequate on both the descriptive and normative levels. Ackerman accordingly proposed a "scientific policymaking" approach to the takings issue. This approach would be conducted on the basis of a complete theory, or "comprehensive view," and much of Ackerman's book was devoted to developing such a theory with the aid of utilitarian and Kantian philosophy. In later books, Ackerman has offered grand theoretical accounts of social justice and, more recently, constitutional law and interpretation.[7]

Although Ackerman may be an extreme case, his attraction to theory is typical of much prominent constitutional scholarship. Drawing on the work of thinkers such as Locke, Kant, Mill, and Rawls, constitutional scholars have worked to elaborate theories of free speech, equality, privacy, representation, and property. Thus, in attempting to articulate a theory that would spell out the proper relationship between government and religion, or that would identify and elaborate the most attractive principle of religious freedom, scholars have been acting as part of a broad movement in legal thought.

Is Theory Unavoidable?

To many scholars, the resort to theory and political philosophy may have seemed—may *still* seem—almost inevitable. If the constitutional text and historical evidence fail to establish any clear meaning for a constitutional provision—and for the Constitution's grander provisions, at least, this failure seems undeniable—then what other alternative do constitutional lawyers have?

The question deserves serious attention. Can we, as a character in Voltaire's *Candide* counseled, "live without theorizing?" In life, as in law, we are constantly confronted with questions that we cannot avoid but for which there is, on the face of things, no obviously right answer. Opinions differ. Authorities seem to conflict. Isn't it inevitable that in these situations we must go beyond surface considerations and try to develop a "theory" to explain which among the competing opinions and authorities we ought to accept?

Before assenting to this claim of necessity, consider a common situation. Leaving work one day, you remark to your associates that you are going to the movies that night. A friend replies, "That's nice. Which show are you going to see?" There are two recent releases—*Batbuster VI* and *Night of the Lizard*—that seem to be the best candidates, but you only say that you haven't decided yet which show to see.

The next day you mention that you went to *Batbuster*. Suppose that your friend now asks, "What's your theory that led you to choose *Batbuster* rather than *Lizard*?" The question would probably seem odd. If your friend insisted on pressing the question in those terms, you might confess that your choice was not dictated by *any* theory, and that in fact you don't even have a theory—not even a sketchy or simplistic or half-baked one—of movie selection. Although there was no clearly correct decision, you nonetheless made a choice without resorting to any theory.

This admission would not mean that you acted without reasons. If instead of inquiring about your "theory," your friend asked simply, "Why did you choose that movie?" you would find the question more natural, and you would probably have no difficulty in answering. Someone might suggest that your reasons express an unarticulated, perhaps subconscious "theory" of movie selection. But this characterization is dubious because there is no basis to assume that your reasons add up to or reflect any coherent pattern or method for choosing movies. Some of your reasons ("Oh, I just felt like it") seem too specific, and too whimsical, to represent any general theory. (Imagine how a similar explanation would sound if offered as part of a scientific or economic theory: "Harvard economist Leonard Lardner has developed a theory of real estate markets which hypothesizes that housing starts are likely to jump dramatically under conditions in which people 'just feel like' buying houses.") Other reasons *might* be generalizable, but there is no assurance that this is the case. You might say, "I went to *Batbuster* because Michael Onegrin was in it." But last month you passed up an Onegrin film to see another show starring no one you'd heard of—just because you felt in the mood for a thriller, or didn't want to drive too far, or couldn't make the earlier showing, or liked the advertisements, or went with a friend who wanted to see it, or . . .

Upon reflection, it seems that most of the decisions we make are more like movie selections than like "theory"-driven decisions. There is no clearly correct answer, and yet we make a choice. We may think and give reasons (although it would be wrong to suppose that these conscious factors are the exclusive, or perhaps even the most important, influences on our behavior). We may even invoke general guidelines or maxims that might be loosely described as "principles," but we do not assume that these guidelines fit nicely together into any complete and internally consistent framework from which we can deduce right answers. In short, our choices do not depend on anything resembling a "theory"—unless, that is, the term is stretched so far as to lose its meaning.

We have a variety of terms that we associate with aspects of this nontheoretical approach: judgment, intuition, instinct, "gut feeling," "muddling through," ad hoc or prudential or pragmatic or contextual decision making. It is possible that the difference between our theoretical and our more nontheoretical activities is a matter of degree rather than a clear, categorical distinction. Nonetheless, our familiarity with and frequent resort to terms describing the nontheoretical approach reveal our sense and understanding that many of our activities and practices are not, and perhaps could not be, governed by any theory. Even if an ambitious social scientist or philosopher, perhaps with the aid of a computer, could develop a complex theoretical model for describing our decisions in these areas, in

practice we do not and probably could not make decisions by refer-
ring to any such model.

For present purposes, it may be helpful to have a single term
for these nontheoretical alternatives. I will refer to them as the "prudential" approach.

Prudence or Theory?

To say that "prudentialism" is a possible alternative to theorizing
does not mean, of course, that the alternative is an attractive one.
The prudential approach is admittedly an untidy way of making
choices; it does not provide the secure sense of certainty and predict-
ability that theory seems to offer. For legal scholars especially, there
are reasons to be wary of prudentialism. After all, to embrace a
prudentialist view of law may require giving up on the aspiration to
see law as a comprehensible and coherent whole or as a "science."

This is not merely an abstract loss. On the practical level, what
kinds of articles would the prudentialist legal scholar write? How
would she go about criticizing or prescribing the decision in a case,
for example, if it is understood that the decision is and should be
determined largely by contextual factors that the judge and the liti-
gants may know first-hand but that are mostly invisible to the
scholar who sits at a distance in the comfort of her office?

Prudentialism also poses a special problem for the constitutional
scholar or the judge who is attached to the institution of judicial
review. In a system that aspires to be democratic, the "countermajoritarian difficulty"[8] — that is, the dubious legitimacy of unelected
judges striking down laws passed by elected representatives — is a
familiar concern. One way of dealing with this difficulty has been
to conceive of constitutional law as an expression of "principles" —
principles that can be fully articulated and developed through theoretical analysis. That kind of theoretical analysis, it has seemed, is a
function that judges — and even more clearly, legal scholars — might
be well situated to perform. On the other hand, if constitutional law
is viewed more as a prudential matter, it becomes much less clear
why judges — and, a fortiori, legal scholars — have any special apti-
tude for making or discerning it.

Not surprisingly, therefore, constitutional scholars have recognized for at least a generation or so the intimate connection between
judicial review and "principle."[9] And "principle," in turn, usually
seems to imply theory. For all these reasons, the scholarly effort

to develop a "theory" of religious freedom is understandable and attractive. [10]

Is Theory Possible?

To *want* a theory, however, or even to "need" one, is not to ensure that an adequate theory is available. A variety of factors may preclude the development of a plausible theory for a given subject matter and thereby relegate that area, for better or worse, to the realm of "muddling through," or of prudentialism. As noted above, most of our personal decisions — selecting a movie, choosing a career, deciding whether to marry or have children — do not seem to lend themselves to resolution through the application of any theory. [11] The same is true for many, perhaps most, political decisions. Although we actively consider and debate *reasons* for adopting particular policies dealing with foreign relations, or taxation, or labor-management disagreements, or welfare, we also recognize that these decisions are ultimately prudential in nature; whether to declare war or raise taxes is a decision that cannot be made simply by slapping down some *theory* or *principle*.

In the ensuing chapters I will suggest that religious freedom is likewise, for better or worse, a prudential matter. My purpose is not exactly to *advocate* a prudential approach to religious freedom or to argue that we ought to choose a prudential over a more theoretical approach. If any plausible theory of religious freedom were available, it would be possible to debate the virtues and advantages of following the prescriptions of that theory or, instead, of adopting a more ad hoc, prudential approach. But we do not have the luxury of that choice. Much as we might want some general theory specifying the proper relationship between government and religion, no adequate theory is or will be forthcoming. That relationship is sensibly governed, rather, by judgments based on shifting conditions and concerns, and these judgments cannot sensibly be reduced to any governing principle or domesticated under the roof of any theory. So if this argument is persuasive, then it seems that our choice, to the extent we have one, is between adopting a constitutional principle based on *bad theory* or, instead, pursuing a more prudential approach.

It may be helpful at the outset to clarify the scope of this argument. A good deal of academic commentary criticizes one or another specific principle or theory of religious freedom — the "no aid" principle, or the "endorsement" theory, or the "accommodation" principle. On a broader scale, some legal scholars, working under the heading of "legal pragmatism,"[12] have recently expressed doubts about the value or possibility of legal theory generally; the pragmatists' objections constitute an effort to achieve "freedom from theory-guilt."[13] In the past, I have engaged in the first kind of criticism[14] and questioned the second.[15] The present discussion, however, is intended to fall in between these positions in its scope. Although I will incidentally criticize some specific theories and principles of religious freedom, this criticism is meant to be illustrative; my broader aim is to show that no adequate theory or principle of religious freedom is possible. At the same time, I do not want to deny in any universal way that "theory" may be possible and desirable in the law; my challenge here is directed only to theories of religious freedom.

6

The Fundamental Conundrum

Any effort to articulate a theory of religious freedom, I will argue in this chapter, founders on a basic theoretical conundrum. The function of a theory of religious freedom is to mediate among a variety of competing religious and secular positions and interests, or to explain how government ought to deal with these competing positions and interests. To perform that function, however, the theory will tacitly but inevitably privilege, or prefer in advance, one of those positions while rejecting or discounting others. But a theory that privileges one of the competing positions and rejects others a priori is not truly a theory of religious freedom at all—or, at least, it is not the sort of theory that modern proponents of religious freedom have sought to develop. This is a simple statement of the conundrum; my purpose in this chapter is to elaborate the problem.

The Impossibility of an Autonomous Theory

The argument must begin by emphasizing a fact that is perhaps obvious but is also, I think, underappreciated: Theories of religious freedom are not self-subsistent, nor are they created ex nihilo. A theory of religious freedom is not sound or unsound, convincing or unconvincing, in the abstract. Rather, any account of religious freedom will necessarily depend on—and hence will stand or fall along with—more basic background beliefs concerning matters of religion and theology, the proper role of government, and "human nature."[1]

This observation is not especially startling, and it may not seem especially troubling either. I will argue, however, that the dependency of theories of religious freedom on background premises or beliefs poses an insuperable obstacle to the development of any theory of religious freedom of the kind that modern scholars have aspired to supply. Because my argument hinges on the impossibility of an autonomous theory, it is important to consider more closely the way in which theories of religious freedom are dependent on background assumptions before discussing the consequences of this dependency.

John Locke's influential argument for religious toleration can serve as an illustration. In "A Letter Concerning Toleration," Locke sets out "to distinguish exactly the business of civil government from that of religion, and to settle the just bounds that lie between the one and the other."[2] The "business of civil government," he asserts, is to care for "civil interests" or, in other words, the "things belonging to this life"; these include "life, liberty, health, and indolence of body; and the possession of outward things, such as money, land, houses, furniture, and the like."[3] Conversely, civil government has no interest in or jurisdiction over the "care of souls," which is the concern of the church. The principal reason for this restriction is straightforward: Government *should not* attempt to care for souls because it simply *has no power* to do so.

> The care of souls cannot belong to the civil magistrate, because his power consists only in outward force: but true and saving religion consists in the inward persuasion of the mind, without which nothing can be acceptable to God. And such is the nature of the understanding, that it cannot be compelled to the belief of anything by outward force.[4]

Although Locke gives other arguments, including familiar modern arguments based on fallibility[5] and the dangers of civil strife,[6] he constantly and primarily recurs to this argument about the impossibility and the religious inefficacy of compelled belief.[7]

This reasoning leads Locke at one point to the confident pronouncement that church and commonwealth are "perfectly distinct, and infinitely different from each other" and that "[t]he boundaries on both sides are fixed and immoveable."[8] But the jurisdictional line becomes blurred somewhat as the essay proceeds, because jurisdictions overlap regarding the not insignificant matter of morality.[9] Because morality concerns the care of souls but also affects civil interests, government in this area may limit religious freedom in ways that may seem objectionable from a modern liberal perspective. For example, Locke holds that government need not tolerate "a Mahometan," because he will inevitably be loyal to a foreign prince.[10] Likewise, atheists are not entitled to toleration because, by denying the existence of God, they undermine the sanctity of "[p]romises, covenants, and oaths, which are the bonds of human society."[11]

These restrictions may lead modern readers to conclude that Locke failed to press his argument to its full conclusion; his position, although perhaps an advance over then prevailing ways of thinking and important for its influence on American statesmen like Jefferson, still seems timid or shortsighted.[12] But this assessment is off the mark. The restrictions Locke allows are in fact consistent with his premises—with the same premises, that is, which permit him to argue for a measure of religious freedom broader in scope than what was then generally accepted. We can, of course, criticize Locke's entire account, including the restrictions he allows, by challenging his premises. And those premises are indeed highly vulnerable to challenge. But challenging those premises undermines not only Locke's restrictions on religious toleration but also his rationale for toleration itself.

Consider more closely the premises, or background beliefs, on which Locke's argument rests. First, he makes assumptions about religion and theology. He assumes that salvation must be achieved by a faith that is purely voluntary. Locke also adopts an otherworldly view of the church and its purpose: "The only business of the church," he insists, "is the salvation of souls."[13] In addition, Locke expresses a latitudinarian theology. He has no patience for dogma and ritual, which in his view are largely irrelevant to salvation; what matters is sincere belief, virtuous conduct, and charity and tolerance toward others—not rites and doctrinal articles of faith.[14]

Locke's argument also presupposes a narrow, essentially laissez-faire view of the proper functions of civil government. The domain of interests that government can legitimately promote is limited,[15] and even within this domain government must avoid paternalistic measures. For example, even though health and physical well-being are within government's jurisdiction, no one should be forced to be healthy against his will or protected against his own negligence.[16] Pernicious or degrading practices are not to be regulated unless they are "prejudicial to other men's rights" or "break the public peace."[17]

Finally, Locke's essay rests on an image of a society composed of essentially self-sufficient individuals. This observation is true in at least two senses. First, Locke pays little or no attention to what might be called the values of community except as these are instrumental to the maintenance of life and property by individuals. Second, Locke assumes that human beings have an inner realm of beliefs that are formed by individual reflection on evidence and reasons and that are impervious to outside coercion. The magistrate may seek to influence this inner realm of beliefs by persuasion and argumentation, but coercive measures will have no effect on them.[18]

Once these background beliefs are made explicit, it is apparent that all are highly controversial. Locke's insistence that the church's concerns are wholly otherworldly contradicts dominant views in the European background against which Locke wrote; it is also inconsistent with the role churches have played in American history.[19] The Social Gospel movement, for example, has had exactly the opposite emphasis: Vital religion must be relevant to, and must seek to improve, the concerns and conditions of *this* life.[20] Locke's latitudinarian view, by disparaging both dogma and ritual, diverges dramatically from the positions held by numerous religious believers throughout history. His restrictive view of the state's functions is likewise incongruent with the role governments have come to play in most modern societies, including ours; and his neglect of community values arguably slights an essential realm of human concerns.

As Locke's background beliefs come to be seen as dubious, his argument for religious tolerance loses force. Locke's libertarian vision suggests that however troubling or offensive a person's religious beliefs may be to others, the community and the state simply have no legitimate interest that might support regulation of those beliefs; and in any case they literally have no power to change the dissenter's views—except, perhaps, by persuasion. But as Locke's individualistic viewpoint is relaxed, the case becomes more complicated. To be sure, the dissenter's obnoxious views may not immediately threaten the property or bodily integrity of others, but they surely do influence the nature of the community that the citizens share. Even while acknowledging that they cannot turn a neighbor from heresy by force, for example, citizens in a community might plausibly fear that if tolerated, the heretic will infect others—their own children, perhaps—who would otherwise be satisfied with the orthodox faith.

Such a development would not only threaten the spiritual welfare of those who (from the orthodox perspective) are thus deceived but might undermine the unity of the community as well. For example, the emergence of dissenters might easily impinge on matters of public schooling, or on marriage practices, or on familial harmony.

In addition, as the notion of the self-sufficient individual becomes problematic, the line between persuasion and coercion seems neither so plain nor so sacred. Many beliefs that human beings sincerely hold may have been shaped by coercion at some point. Augustine affirmed, as did Locke, that ultimately only a genuine faith can save; but he also recognized (as parents often do, and as our modern system of compulsory schooling arguably does) that coercive measures *can* sometimes put a person in a position from which he can favorably consider, and perhaps come to embrace, a true idea. Augustine cited the example of the Apostle Paul, who while engaged in the persecution of Christians was converted by being temporarily struck blind; God had "not only compelled Paul . . . by word but He also prostrated him with power, and in order to lead him from the savagery of his dark unbeliefs to the desire of the light of the heart, he first struck him with bodily blindness."[21]

The object of this discussion is not to determine whether either Locke's premises or his conclusions are sound or not. The point, rather, is that Locke's account of religious toleration is dependent on background beliefs about religion, government, society, and human psychology. These background beliefs generate both the rationale for and the restrictions on religious toleration. If one accepts all of Locke's background beliefs, his arguments for religious toleration (and for particular limitations on such toleration) will likely seem attractive. If one rejects one or more of those background beliefs, the argument will come to lose its force.[22]

In this respect, Locke's account is like any other account of religious freedom. Theories of religious freedom will always rest on background beliefs that provide reasons for tolerating or protecting some aspects of religious practice and for regulating other aspects. Indeed, an account of religious freedom that was simply asserted and not justified by reference to supporting premises would be mere fiat, and hence could hardly be counted as a theory at all.[23] And it follows that a theoretical account of religious freedom cannot be assessed in the abstract; it must be considered with the background beliefs that support it, and it will be convincing only insofar as those supporting beliefs are themselves convincing.

The "Preferred Position" Approach

Upon reflection, the dependency of theory on background beliefs is not surprising. After all, how could anyone expect to go about developing a theory of religious freedom without invoking assumptions about, for example, the proper functions of government, the nature of religion, and the question of what is valuable for human beings? But the dependency of theory on background beliefs leads directly to the conundrum noted at the beginning of this chapter. [24]

The problem, simply put, is that theories of religious freedom seek to reconcile or to mediate among competing religious and secular positions within a society, but those competing positions disagree about the very background beliefs on which a theory of religious freedom must rest. One religion will maintain beliefs about theology, government, and human nature that may support a particular version of religious freedom. A different religion or a secular viewpoint will support different background beliefs that logically generate different views or theories of religious freedom. In adopting a theory of religious freedom that is consistent with some background beliefs but not with others, therefore, government (or the judge or the legal scholar) must adopt, or privilege, one of the competing secular or religious positions. Yet this adopting or preferring of one religious or secular position over its competitors is precisely what modern theories of religious freedom seek to avoid. [25] Hence, theories of religious freedom can function only by implicitly betraying their own objective.

To appreciate this difficulty, consider a simple community in which all citizens hold to one of four positions, of which two are religious and two are secular. We may call these groups of citizens the religious voluntarists, the religious behaviorists, the secular pessimists, and the secular optimists.

The religious voluntarists believe that this life is merely an eyeblink in the vast expanse of eternity; consequently, eternal goods— above all, the salvation of souls— are of infinitely greater value than all imaginable earthly benefits. "For what shall it profit a man, if he shall gain the whole world, and lose his own soul?" [26] Voluntarists also believe that individuals attain salvation only by living strictly in accordance with the dictates of conscience. Consistent with these beliefs, the voluntarists have a very limited view of the proper functions of government. The main purpose of government, they maintain, is to protect religious freedom and to maintain civil peace so that citizens will be free to act in accordance with their religious convictions.

The religious behaviorists agree on the overriding importance of eternal as opposed to temporal goods. Unlike the voluntarists, however, the behaviorists believe that salvation is attained by behaving in conformity to particular divine laws, including laws prescribing the performance of certain religious rites. In this more legalistic view, a person's *motive* for behaving (or *not* behaving) in the proper way is not ultimately dispositive: Individuals who doubtfully and reluctantly behave in the right way will nonetheless go to heaven, whereas those who with the purest of intentions transgress the divine law will go to hell (just as citizens who violate the criminal law for what they think are worthy reasons still may wind up in jail). Consequently, the behaviorists see greater scope for governmental action; the judicious use of coercion to prevent citizens from straying might produce eternal benefits.

In contrast to the religious groups, both the secular pessimists and the secular optimists believe that the goods of this life are the only goods there are. These groups, as the poem says, will take the cash and let the credit go; they will not sigh for the prophet's paradise to come. But the secular groups diverge over another issue: the efficacy of collective or state action. The pessimists are quite despairing about the possibility of accomplishing any good through collective action, and they suspect that terms such as *public interest* and *common good* are little more than mystical and potentially mischievous nonsense. The optimists, by contrast, are convinced that collective action can and should be liberally used to promote social welfare.

Now consider how these various groups will react to two different claims sounding in "religious freedom." The first claim involves a man — call him George Reynolds[27] — who contends that his sincere religious conviction requires him to marry more than one wife, even though bigamy laws prohibit such behavior. The second claimant, whom we may call Jonas Yoder,[28] asserts that he cannot in good conscience comply with laws requiring him to send his children to school beyond a certain age because school will corrupt them and undermine their religious faith.

The religious voluntarists would likely favor Reynolds's claim. Since Reynolds is acting in accordance with his religious convictions in taking more than one wife, there would be no spiritual benefit but would be tremendous spiritual cost in forcing him to remain monogamous. Even if monogamy is more consistent with temporal welfare (perhaps because it promotes democracy and social stability),[29] no temporal benefit could compensate for the loss of Reynolds's soul.

The secular pessimists might join in this conclusion but for a different reason. They regard Reynolds's beliefs as false and perhaps contemptible; still, their gloomy view of collective action leads them to a libertarian position that would not permit government, in a misguided effort to further the general welfare, to forbid marital arrangements among consenting adults.[30]

The religious behaviorists, by contrast, would reject Reynolds's claim if they believe monogamy is divinely prescribed; indeed, they would likely enforce monogamy even at the cost of disrupting civil peace. The secular optimists might also reject the religious-freedom claim, but only if they believe (as we may suppose they do) that polygamy is injurious to temporal interests.

Both the religious voluntarists and the secular pessimists might also side with Jonas Yoder, albeit again for very different reasons and with different consequences. For example, the pessimists' libertarian rationale might also lead them to exempt a secular objector to forced education — Henry David Thoreau, for example[31] — while the voluntarists would afford no special respect to a purely secular claim. The religious behaviorists' position would turn on whether they think the education imposed by the state induces behavior that is consistent with the divine law, while the secular optimists would likely place overriding value on the goods to be achieved by the state-imposed requirement of education.

Not surprisingly, therefore, different background beliefs dictate different responses to these claims of religious freedom. The critical question at this point is whether it is possible to articulate a theory of religious freedom that would somehow transcend these disagreements and prescribe how the conflicts should be resolved. In other words, can the state, or the theorist, answer questions about religious freedom without consciously or implicitly adopting the views of religious voluntarism, religious behaviorism, secular optimism, or secular pessimism as the perspective from which competing claims are to be judged?

It is hard to see how this could be done. Indeed, what could a theorist possibly do other than adopt one or another of the competing sets of background beliefs, thereby situating herself *within* the dispute, rather than above or outside it? It is impossible, as argued above, to develop a theory of religious freedom *without* background beliefs or premises. Nor does it seem possible to premise a theory of religious freedom on background beliefs that are independent of the basic competing religious and secular positions within the community. The theorist, after all, is herself part of the community; hence, her own beliefs will ipso facto represent one position within the community. Moreover, even if it were somehow possible to articulate a theory of religious freedom based on premises that do not correspond to the beliefs of any of the competing positions within a community, why would that course be attractive? What would be the sense of resolving conflicts in accordance with a theory based on premises that *no one* within the community accepts? It seems, therefore, that the theorist has no choice but to develop a theory based on background beliefs held by one (or perhaps, at least for some issues, a convergence of more than one) of the competing positions within the community. We may refer to this course as the "preferred position" approach to theorizing.

Problems with the "Preferred Position" Approach

The discussion thus far suggests that theorizing about religious freedom will necessarily adopt a preferred position approach. But this approach, however inevitable, is also subject to vitiating questions and objections.

First, how does the theorist select the preferred position whose beliefs she will use as premises for her theory? Perhaps the most obvious answer is that the theorist will choose the position that she believes to be the most true, or plausible, or theoretically attractive. If the theorist takes this course, however, then debates about religious freedom will entail, and depend on, debates about the truth or attractiveness of the competing religious or secular positions themselves.

To simplify greatly, we might have Catholic and Protestant and Deweyan and Marxist theories of religious freedom.[32] Insofar as it is consistently and carefully developed, each of these theories would be plausible *if* the underlying position that generates the theory is itself plausible. To select the most plausible theory of religious freedom, therefore, we would have to debate and choose among the Catholic, Protestant, Deweyan, and Marxist "faiths." But this conclusion is disconcerting. To say that a theory of religious freedom requires the theorist to determine which of the conflicting religious or secular positions within a society is most plausible or attractive seems to defeat the purpose that prompted the theorist to seek a theory of religious freedom in the first place.

Alternatively, a theorist might defend her preferred position by arguing not that the position is the best or most true in any general or abstract sense, but rather that it is the position commanded by the Constitution. Contemporary constitutional scholars who adopt a secular perspective in discussing the meaning and scope of religious freedom would likely take this stance. The meaning of the First Amendment must be elaborated in accordance with secular criteria, they might say, not because a secular worldview is "true" and a religious worldview is "false," but simply because the Constitution requires government to be secular. [33]

But this attempt to avoid deciding on the truth or attractiveness of the basic conflicting positions generates a dilemma. If the proposition that a particular position should be preferred because it is the one commanded by the Constitution is intended as a statement about "original meaning,"[34] then that proposition is unpersuasive; it is subject to all the objections discussed in the preceding chapters. The Constitution simply did not say that questions of religious freedom must be resolved from a secular (or a religious) perspective; it offered no substantive guidance on this subject. [35]

Conversely, if the proposition is *not* intended as an assertion about original meaning, then how is it to be understood? Perhaps the theorist would respond that the Constitution *should* be interpreted to require a particular basic perspective—a secular perspective, for example. But *why* should the Constitution be interpreted in this way? Someone might believe, of course, that viewing the Constitution as a secular document will make it, to borrow a phrase, "the best it can be." And from a secular perspective—that is, a perspective that prefers secular beliefs and values—this conclusion is probably correct. But this observation merely pushes the question back a step: Why should we adopt a secular perspective in determining what will make the Constitution the best it can be?

There seems to be no good answer to this question. If the response is that secular values and beliefs are superior to religious values and beliefs, then the theorist has simply reverted to the alternative discussed above—the alternative, that is, of selecting the truest or best position—and hence must confront the same problems discussed earlier. In the alternative, a proponent of the secular perspective might assert that the beliefs and values of American citizens require a secular perspective, but this assertion is almost surely wrong as an empirical matter. [36] Finally, if the answer is that a secular perspective is appropriate because the Constitution commands that perspective, the argument is plainly circular. It says, in essence, that we should treat the Constitution as privileging a secular position because the Constitution privileges a secular position.

Even if the problem of selecting a preferred position could be satisfactorily solved, a related question would then arise: Should a preferred position theory "count" as a genuine theory of religious freedom at all? If it could be developed, such a theory *would*, to be sure, specify certain areas in which the preferred position leaves individuals free to make religious choices. Still, there is something odd about calling this a theory *of religious freedom*, since the freedom granted is much like the freedom recognized by a dictator who insists, "My subjects are perfectly free to do as they choose as long as they do nothing that I forbid." The preferred position approach brings to mind Winston Churchill's statement that "[i]n England there is absolute freedom of speech as long as the speech does not violate the law" — a statement that Frederick Schauer has aptly described as "profoundly silly."[37]

This objection might be put in a different way: Rather than being characterized as a theory of "religious freedom," the preferred position theory might be called a theory of "tolerance." By determining the scope of religious freedom in accordance with the criteria or values of a preferred religious or secular position, this kind of theory effectively rejects on the most basic level — on the "constitutional" or "constitutive" level — the contrary secular and religious positions whose criteria or values were *not* selected as the foundation for constitutional theorizing, even though the theory may tolerate those unapproved beliefs and practices on a different level. But a theory of religious tolerance would be subject to the objections that Thomas Paine, James Madison, and others have made against mere religious "toleration."[38] Paine argued, for example, that "[t]oleration is not the *opposite* of intoleration, but is the *counterfeit* of it. Both are despotisms."[39] In framing Virginia's Declaration of Rights, Madison objected to George Mason's proposal that "all men should enjoy the fullest Toleration in the Exercise of Religion according to the Dictates of Conscience"; Madison offered an amendment "eliminating 'toleration' and putting in its place that 'all men are equally entitled to the full and free exercise of religion according to the dictates of conscience.'"[40] Philip Kurland asserts the plausible and commonly accepted distinction: Religious toleration is not equivalent to religious freedom because unlike toleration, which implies a preferred or orthodox position that "puts up with" other, less-favored views, religious freedom entails that "all religions are equal in the eyes of the law."[41]

Indeed, a theory derived from the preferred position might as accurately be called a theory of "official orthodoxy" or of religious or secular "establishment."[42] The theory in essence asserts (or assumes) that government should operate in accordance with the standards and values of some religious or secular orthodoxy and should grant dissenters the freedom to deviate from the orthodoxy only insofar as the orthodoxy itself allows.

In advocating a secular baseline, Kathleen Sullivan is straight-forward in acknowledging this fact. The Constitution effected, she says in a recurring and hence apparently calculated phrase, "the *establishment* of the secular public order."[43] The Constitution does not command "nonestablishment," in other words; it decrees a secular "establishment." Under this secular establishment, religious freedom encompasses only "the exercise of religious liberty *insofar as compatible with the establishment of the secular public order.*"[44] For example, if the exercise of religion results in disabilities, such as the exclusion of religious believers or institutions from public benefits or programs, that result is natural and unobjectionable. Such exclusion is "man-dated by the Establishment Clause"—meaning, of course, the "secu-lar establishment" clause. This clause "will often require excluding religious organizations from public programs, or will necessitate religion-restrictive conditions on their participation."[45]

Sullivan accurately describes the consequences of privileging a secular position; the question is whether this position can plausibly be characterized by the term *religious freedom.* How is Sullivan's secu-lar establishment different with regard to religious freedom than religious establishments have been? Probably no religion has ever purported to prescribe a particular belief on *every* question or a par-ticular course of conduct in *every* matter.[46] Even the most thorough-going religious establishment would allow citizens "the exercise of religious liberty insofar as compatible with the establishment of the [religious] public order." Thus, in merely substituting one kind of establishment for another, Sullivan seems to miss the whole point of theoretical discourse about religious freedom.

Yet if Sullivan's position is objectionable in this respect, it is only because her position openly acknowledges adopting or privileg-ing an orthodoxy. And the preceding discussion suggests that this privileging, although usually concealed, is in fact an inescapable aspect of *any* theory of religious freedom.

It may be helpful to summarize the foregoing argument. The

theorist of religious freedom, it seems, must ground her theory in premises or background beliefs compatible with one (or perhaps, insofar as they sometimes happen to converge, some) of the competing religious or secular positions whose claims a theory of religious freedom seeks to mediate. The theorist in effect adopts one among the competing positions and then grants other faiths only the freedom that the preferred position permits. Whether such a theory deserves to be called a theory of religious freedom at all seems doubtful, and it is certain that modern judges and theorists have aspired to do much more.

They have aspired, more specifically, to develop a theory that is "neutral" as among competing religious and secular positions — neutral, as the Supreme Court has repeatedly put it, both among religions and between religion and nonreligion. The foregoing discussion is in fact an argument against the possibility of a "neutral" theory. However, since judges and legal scholars persist in the belief that religious neutrality is a coherent and attainable ideal, it may be helpful to consider that ideal more closely. That is the task of the next chapter.

7

The Pursuit of Neutrality

Perhaps the most pervasive theme in modern judicial and academic discourse on the subject of religious freedom is "neutrality." The Supreme Court has repeatedly insisted that government must be neutral both among religions and between religion and nonreligion.[1] Scholars have offered myriad explications of the ideal of religious neutrality.[2] Phillip Johnson's observation exaggerates only slightly in describing the breadth of the consensus: "That in some sense the federal government and the states ought to be 'neutral' in religious matters is undisputed."[3]

Without actually using the term, the preceding chapter has already discussed both the necessity and the futility of this quest for neutrality. The aspiration to neutrality can be understood as an effort to avoid or transcend the kind of theorizing that adopts or prefers in advance one of the competing religious or secular positions within a community and then allows other positions only as much freedom as the preferred position prescribes. As discussed, it is questionable whether this kind of preferred position theory can properly be regarded as a theory of "religious freedom" at all. Thus, neutrality is not merely one major theme among others, or one attractive theoretical option, but rather an essential theoretical requirement. A genuine theory of religious freedom, by this view, would of necessity be a "neutral" theory in the sense that it would not begin by adopting or favoring one of the competing religious or secular positions. Unfortunately, since every theory of religious freedom depends on background beliefs that will be derived from and compatible with one or some of those positions but not others, this sort of neutral theory also appears to be unattainable.

Outside the field of religious freedom, legal claims to neutrality have been subjected to considerable criticism in recent decades, and some of this criticism has been applied to the Supreme Court's religion clause jurisprudence as well.[4] But the notion of religious neutrality has remarkable resiliency. Indeed, it would not be much of an overstatement to say that modern legal discourse about religious freedom consists of judges and legal scholars unblushingly proclaiming their "neutrality" even as they reject both the premises and the conclusions of their adversaries. In part, this spectacle reflects the semantic slipperiness of the term. Neutrality, as Justice John Marshall Harlan observed, is "a coat of many colors,"[5] and its multiple meanings provide ample opportunity for equivocation and obfuscation, deliberate or accidental. (This semantic slipperiness is the reason why, in the previous chapter, I have tried to address the problem to which the pursuit of "neutrality" is a response without using the term at all.)

Because the ideal of religious neutrality is at once so ubiquitous and so elusive, it is helpful to consider more closely some of the more common versions of that ideal. Some of these versions, I will argue, may indeed have limited value, but none can solve the conundrum discussed in the preceding chapter.

Neutral Application

Perhaps the most modest version of neutrality uses the concept to describe the uniform or impartial application of a rule or principle according to its own terms. An example may help to clarify this version. Suppose the governor issues an order declaring that all Protestants and no Catholics shall receive a tax credit of $1,000. Among those who apply for the credit are one of the governor's most bitter and powerful political enemies, who happens to be Protestant, and the governor's best friend, who happens to be Catholic. Consistent with his order, the governor instructs that the tax credit be given to his political enemy but not to his best friend.

Has the governor acted "neutrally"? In one sense, it seems, he has. The governor has applied his order according to its terms without regard to extraneous considerations that might be likely to influence him. So he can plausibly claim to have acted "neutrally" in the *application* of the rule.

In this way, the language of neutrality can be helpful in discussing the evenhanded application of a rule, doctrine, or theory. This usage is familiar; it is seemingly this kind of impartial application that we have in mind when we say that a judge should be neutral in trying and deciding a case or that an umpire or referee ought to be neutral in officiating a game.[6] It should also be clear, however, that this version of neutrality does nothing to help the theorist avoid the problem of "preferred position" theorizing. The fact that a rule is neutrally or evenhandedly *applied* does not make the *rule itself* neutral, as the above example shows. Thus, if Catholics protest what they view as an unfair and discriminatory law, the governor's protestation that he has applied the law in strictly neutral fashion would be correct but at the same time wholly beside the point.

Neutrality as Nondiscrimination

The above example may seem to suggest a more useful and substantial version of neutrality: A "neutral" law or theory, we might say, is one that does not disfavor or discriminate against any particular secular or religious position. It seems natural, after all, to say that the hypothetical tax-credit order described above is not "neutral" because it favors Protestants while disfavoring or discriminating against Catholics. Unfortunately, upon inspection, this notion of neutrality as nondiscrimination turns out to be a deceptive way of begging the question.

In both popular and loose legal discourse, saying that a law "discriminates" is virtually equivalent to saying that the law "*wrongfully* discriminates." This equivalence facilitates an appealing but faulty argument. The first step is to say that a law or policy *disfavors* someone. Let us say that it disfavors Jones. This assertion can then be restated in the language of "discrimination": If the law "disfavors" Jones, then it "discriminates against" him. And if the law "discriminates," then is it not unfair or wrongful in its treatment of Jones?

The problem is that we cannot know that a law or policy "wrongfully discriminates" (or, in common usage, simply "discriminates") without presupposing some substantive position or premise that explains how Jones *should* be treated (or at least *to whom* he should be treated similarly, and in what respects).[7] If we are already convinced on other, perhaps unspoken grounds that Jones has been mistreated, we may not object to the easy slippage from "disfavor" to "discriminate" and from "discriminate" to "wrongfully discriminate."

Conversely, if we are *not* already convinced that Jones has been mistreated, the equivocation will be evident. We would hardly be persuaded, for example, by a challenge to a law prohibiting rape if the challenge asserted that the law "discriminates against" rapists. We might respond to this challenge by saying that although the law punishes rapists and thus treats them less favorably than nonrapists, it does not "discriminate" against them, but rather treats them as they deserve. Or if someone insisted on using the term *discrimination*, then we might simply observe that this kind of discrimination, if it can be called that, is entirely appropriate.

The point is that the language of "discrimination" or disadvantaging does not obviate, but rather presupposes, a substantive standard for determining how conflicting claims or interests should be treated. More generally, it is the business of government to make distinctions, to grant some claims and deny others, and in that sense to disfavor some individuals and groups while favoring others. How government should perform this business is a difficult question that cannot be answered simply by invoking the language of "disfavoring" or "discrimination."

With respect to religion, more specifically, it is arguable that government *should* treat religious claims and interests differently than it treats analogous nonreligious claims and interests. In some contexts, the differential treatment might be beneficial to religion. Perhaps it is appropriate, for example, that persons who for religious reasons cannot accept available employment should still be eligible for unemployment compensation but that persons who decline employment for purely secular reasons should lose this eligibility.[8] In other contexts, appropriate differential treatment might disfavor or disadvantage religion. It may be proper for government to subsidize universities, farmers, and artists but not churches.[9] In any case, whether differential treatment is appropriate or not depends on the premises, or background beliefs, that we bring to the question.

In short, if the assertion that a particular law disfavors or discriminates against (or in favor of) religion is intended as a purely factual, nonjudgmental description, then a sufficiently precise assertion might be accurate in a given context, but it fails to answer the ultimate question: Is this kind of disfavoring or discrimination appropriate? Conversely, if the assertion is intended (as it typically is) to convey a judgment of disapproval, then the assertion does not avoid, but merely obscures, the problem of selecting background beliefs, or of choosing a preferred position, by which to decide whether a particular kind or instance of differential treatment is appropriate or not.

This analysis of neutrality as nondiscrimination applies, I believe, to the "substantive neutrality" advocated by Douglas Laycock. [10] In Laycock's view, neutrality means that "the religion clauses require government to minimize the extent to which it either encourages or discourages religious belief or disbelief, practice or nonpractice, observance or nonobservance." [11] Government must not try to influence religious beliefs or choices "either by coercion or by persuasion." [12] The background premises that inform Laycock's conception appear to include the premises (*a*) that religious beliefs and practices are valuable and deserving of greater respect than many other kinds of beliefs and practices toward which governmental "neutrality" is *not* required (*b*) but only if religious beliefs and practices are voluntarily chosen — in a very strong (and somewhat underspecified) sense of "voluntariness." [13]

The problem with these background beliefs is not that they are necessarily or plainly false; indeed, I myself happen to agree that (*a*) and something like (*b*) are correct. I say "happen to agree," though, because of course there are many other, inconsistent alternatives that some people in our society favor. One might reject (*a*), for example, in favor of the view that religious choices are no more worthy of respect and protection than other personal choices. Indeed, one might believe (and many do) that religion is on the whole an unfortunate or even pernicious aspect of our culture — one that we ought to at least gently discourage. [14] Conversely, one might believe that religion is a human or social good that government should actively promote — at least through "persuasion." [15] With regard to premise (*b*), Laycock's assumption that even "persuasion" unduly undermines the voluntariness of religious choice is dubious. Locke, for example, while insisting that religious faith must be strictly voluntary, explicitly allowed for governmental persuasion in matters of religion. [16] Hence, Laycock's version of "neutrality" may be attractive, but it clearly is not "neutral" with respect to potential background beliefs that might inform one's views about religious freedom. Rather, Laycock would adopt as constitutional orthodoxy a set of controversial beliefs about the nature and value of religion, the proper function of government, and human psychology.

Secularism as Neutrality

Perhaps the most common modern version of neutrality holds that government can remain neutral in matters of religion by confining itself to the realm of the secular. Thus, the so-called *Lemon* test, which the courts have applied in establishment clause cases for over two decades, requires that government act for secular purposes and in ways that have primarily secular effects; and the Supreme Court has viewed this doctrine as embodying an ideal of "neutrality."[17] The equation of neutrality and secularism is especially conspicuous in cases dealing with public schools; the gravamen of a long line of decisions is that the public-school curricula should be scrupulously neutral in matters of religion and that the schools comply with this obligation by teaching a strictly secular curriculum. If religious materials are used at all, they must be used in an "objective" or "secular" way.[18] In theory, for example, students might be allowed to study the Bible but only if they study it as literature or history, not as scripture.[19]

Although deeply entrenched in modern legal discourse, this equation of secularism and neutrality is also curious. One need not suppose any implacable, across-the-board enmity between the religious and the secular to appreciate that in many contexts and on many issues some widely held religious values and beliefs are directly at odds with secular values and beliefs. Religion and secularism are not invariably foes, but sometimes they are antagonistic;[20] and even in more peaceful settings they are, often enough, mutually suspicious competitors. Hence, the recurring pronouncement that the schools must be neutral *and therefore* entirely secular is much like an announcement, made by the president of the company: "In hiring employees this company will be strictly nonpartisan, and therefore we will hire only Republicans." What is puzzling is that a host of judges and legal scholars can take such professions of neutrality seriously.[21]

Not surprisingly, the attempt to maintain the equation of state neutrality and state secularism sometimes creates embarrassing perplexities in legal reasoning. In *Epperson v. Arkansas*,[22] for example, the Supreme Court invalidated an old and practically defunct Tennessee law that prohibited the teaching of evolution in public schools. In explaining its decision, the Court emphasized the imperative of neutrality: "Government in our democracy, state and national, must be neutral in matters of religious theory, doctrine, and practice. It may not be hostile to any religion or to the advocacy of no-religion."[23] Later in the opinion the Court returned to this theme, again insisting that "the State may not adopt programs or practices in its public schools or colleges which 'aid or oppose' any religion. *This prohibition is absolute*."[24] The Court was also convinced that the theory of evolution contradicts some persons' religious beliefs about the origins of humankind and that this inconsistency was

the reason for the Tennessee law.[25] On this basis the Court ruled
the law unconstitutional.

Read in this way, the Court's opinion seems to have almost
syllogistic force. One might present the syllogism as follows:

1. The constitutional requirement of religious neutrality absolutely prohibits the state from either aiding or opposing any
   religious belief in the public schools.
2. A law forbidding the teaching of evolution aids some (fundamentalist) religious beliefs.[26]
3. Therefore, the constitutional requirement of religious neutrality absolutely prohibits the state from enacting a law
   forbidding the teaching of evolution in the public schools.

Unfortunately, using nothing but the Court's own assertions
one can construct a countersyllogism of equal force:

1. The constitutional requirement of religious neutrality absolutely prohibits the state from either aiding or opposing any
   religious belief in the public schools.
2. The theory of evolution contradicts, and thus opposes, some
   (fundamentalist) religious beliefs.
3. Therefore, the constitutional requirement of religious neutrality absolutely prohibits the state from teaching evolution
   in the public schools.

In sum, the Court's own pronouncements logically show (a) that the
state cannot forbid the teaching of evolution and (b) that the state
cannot teach evolution (or that *the Constitution itself* forbids the teaching of evolution).

One might try to avoid this predicament by focusing not on the
effects of teaching or not teaching evolution, but rather on the *motives*
that are thought to produce such actions. If the schools decline to
teach evolution, one might argue, their purpose is to protect and
thus promote fundamentalist religion.[27] By contrast, if the schools
decide to teach evolution, they do so not for the purpose of opposing
fundamentalist religion (although their teaching might well have
that effect); rather, they teach evolution because scientific research
indicates that the theory of evolution is probably "true."

This characterization, however, fails to dissolve the dilemma.
Although the point may be arguable,[28] let us grant that the Tennessee law was adopted at the insistence of religious fundamentalists
who believed, contrary to the theory of evolution, that the world was
created by God in six days. It is nonetheless seriously misleading to
say that Tennessee, or the fundamentalists in Tennessee, favored

the six-day theory *because it is religious*. After all, there are undoubtedly many beliefs — beliefs held by Muslims, Hindus, Buddhists,
and nonfundamentalist Christians, for example — that the fundamentalists would likely consider to be "religious" in nature but also
"false." The fundamentalists surely would not want these false beliefs
propagated in the public schools — even though (or especially because) the beliefs are "religious." If the fundamentalists advocate
that schools promote (or at least not undermine) the six-day theory,
they take that position because they believe the six-day theory is
true. [29] In this respect, they are just like nonfundamentalists who
favor the teaching of evolution, not because they dislike fundamentalists, [30] but because they believe *that theory* is true. [31]

To be sure, the fundamentalists and their critics have very
different approaches to discerning the "truth" in this matter. The
fundamentalists rely on a literal understanding of scripture, while
proponents of evolution favor a secular and scientific method. These
approaches appear to be, in this context at least, incompatible: The
fundamentalist may regard the Bible as infallible, [32] while the ardent
secularist holds that "such things as divine revelation and biblical
literalism are irrational superstitious nonsense." [33] These views plainly reflect very different background beliefs, and there is no apparent
"neutral" way either to reconcile them or to choose between them.
In this controversy, therefore, everything turns on which set of background beliefs one subscribes to.

The Supreme Court chose to subscribe to a secular position.
The merits of that choice are not at issue here; the point, rather, is
that only a curious kind of self-delusion could lead anyone to assert,
as the *Epperson* majority did with such fervor, that the choice of a
secular position was a "neutral" one that did not either "aid or oppose" any religion. It is immediately obvious, on the contrary, that
the Court's *conclusion* rejected the fundamentalist position; and upon
reflection it is also apparent that in its *premises* the Court had rejected
in advance the fundamentalist position and background beliefs, with
their emphasis on biblical literalism as the avenue to truth. [34] In this
respect, *Epperson* is a microcosm of modern judicial thinking on the
subject of religious neutrality.

A Trichotomy of Values

A different formulation of neutrality might be viewed either as an
attempt to rehabilitate the neutrality-as-secularism theme or per-

haps as an independent version in its own right. This approach attempts to divide the universe of beliefs and values into three categories: religious, irreligious, and nonreligious. The state violates its obligation of neutrality, this position holds, if it acts on either religious or irreligious grounds. But the state can remain neutral by staying within the merely nonreligious domain.[35]

Perhaps the clearest expression of this position was given by Judge William Canby in *Grove v. Mead School District*.[36] In that case, the plaintiffs objected on religion clause grounds to a book, *The Learning Tree*, included in the tenth-grade curriculum. Concurring in a decision rejecting this claim, Canby acknowledged the "sincerity of the plaintiffs' religious objections," and he granted that "the work is antithetical to the particular Christian beliefs espoused by plaintiffs."[37] Nonetheless, Canby concluded that the use of the book was consistent with the school's obligation to be neutral regarding religion. The flaw in the plaintiffs' position, he argued, was its "dualistic social outlook," which "tends to divide the universe of value-laden thought into only two categories—the religious and the anti-religious." Rejecting this dichotomy, Canby asserted that "distinctions must be drawn to recognize not simply 'religious' and 'anti-religious,' but 'non-religious' governmental activity as well."[38]

The bulk of Canby's opinion was devoted to showing that the school's decision to use the book was not antireligious but merely nonreligious. "It is true," he conceded, "that *The Learning Tree* poses questions and ponders doubts with which plaintiffs may be uncomfortable."[39] However, citing Paul Tillich, Canby observed that "[h]onest, even agonizing doubt is not incompatible with Christian theism."[40] Canby also enlisted the authority of other theologians to buttress his position, including Hans Kung, Karl Barth, and Harvey Cox.[41]

Canby's proposed trichotomy may accurately capture assumptions implicit in much legal discourse, including judicial opinions. Indeed, the pervasive equation of "secular" and "neutral," discussed above, seems to reflect some such conception, in which the "secular" is regarded as nonreligious but not irreligious. Nonetheless, the replacement of a dichotomy with respect to religion (pro or con) with a trichotomy (pro or con or neither pro nor con) does not permit the theorist or judge to avoid the problems of "preferred position" theorizing or to achieve any genuine neutrality regarding religion.

One way to appreciate this failure is to ask how we would decide whether a particular controversial book or decision or legisla-

tive purpose fits into the religious, irreligious, or nonreligious category. Canby assumed, for example, that the school's inclusion of
The Learning Tree in the curriculum was merely nonreligious, not
irreligious. From *his* perspective, presumably, this assumption was
true; an examination of the book and its themes was not incompatible, we may suppose, with any religious belief held by Judge Canby.
Moreover, Canby's perspective was consistent with the perspectives
of other religious people such as Tillich, Kung, Barth, and Cox,
whom Canby cited for support.

But of course there are other religious perspectives besides Canby's and Tillich's. It is imaginable, for example, that an admirer of
the book might regard *The Learning Tree* as profoundly religious in
its themes and content, and indeed might want to expose school-
children to it precisely in the hope that they might absorb its religious ideals. Conversely, it is immediately obvious that from the
perspective of the plaintiffs, studying the book was more than a
nonreligious exercise; it was positively contrary, apparently, to *their*
religious values or beliefs, as Canby effectively conceded when he
acknowledged the sincerity of the plaintiffs' religious objections to
the school's use of the book. In concluding that the school's inclusion
of the book was merely nonreligious, therefore, Canby simply privi-
leged his own (and perhaps the school officials') religious perspective
over alternative perspectives, including the perspective of the plaintiffs, and then drew the conclusion that his preferred perspective
dictated.

This privileging was not avoided, but rather was highlighted,
by Canby's citations to authorities like Tillich, Kung, Barth, and
Cox. Indeed, in an opinion that attempted to be serious and sensitive, Canby's confident invocation of these authorities disclosed a
remarkable innocence. If a Quaker or a Baptist raised a religious
objection to a law or practice, would Canby cite a Catholic theolo-
gian to show that "Christian theism" does not support the objection?
If an Orthodox Jew objected to some dietary or dress requirement,[42]
would the judge cite a secular Jewish thinker to show that the requirement is not inconsistent with "Judaism"? Clearly, theologians
like Tillich, Kung, Barth, and Cox are not apt expositors of the
plaintiffs' more fundamentalist faith. Tillich, for example, scorned
that faith with the observation that a fundamentalist is someone who
makes "a theological dogma out of his ignorance."[43] Fundamentalists, for their part, may regard liberal Christians like Tillich as little
better than apostates. And despite Canby's profession of neutrality,
in classifying the school's curricular decision as benignly nonrelig-

ious, his opinion undeniably rejected the plaintiffs' theological perspective, from which the school's program was antireligious, in favor of the more liberal perspective of a Tillich, with its embrace of "honest, agonizing doubt."[44]

A similar analysis could be made of the issue in *Epperson*. Is the theory of evolution religious, or irreligious, or merely nonreligious? To some scientists, evolution is neither religious nor irreligious; it simply does not speak to questions of religion at all.[45] To many fundamentalists, by contrast, this is manifestly not so; the theory of evolution directly contradicts *their* religious beliefs, and hence can hardly be regarded as merely "nonreligious." Of course, some proponents of evolution within the scientific community agree that evolution contradicts religion,[46] and, conversely, a few have elevated evolution to the status of at least a quasi religion[47] — although Supreme Court decisions in this context meticulously overlook these facts.

In sum, carving out a category for the merely "nonreligious" does nothing to obviate the need to adopt or privilege some secular or religious position in assigning particular beliefs, texts, or programs to one of these categories. On the contrary, categorizing a controversial instance presupposes a perspective that in turn reflects the privileging of a position and the implicit rejection of other positions that would prescribe a different classification.

Even more fundamentally, the very decision to divide the universe of beliefs and values into three categories is itself compatible with some background beliefs but not with others. Many religious thinkers have emphatically rejected the religious/neutrally nonreligious/irreligious trichotomy and have held instead that the universe of values constitutes a dichotomy. Values that are not religious are thus necessarily irreligious; individuals who do not embrace the faith thereby reject and oppose it. "He who is not with me is against me." This either/or theme is repeated throughout the New Testament.[48] Richard Niebuhr has observed that such thinking characterized the early Christians, as well as later believers such as the Spiritual Franciscans, George Fox, and Leo Tolstoy.[49] More recently, Malcolm Muggeridge describes the "human drama" as an "obvious dichotomy" shaped by two opposing forces: "One is the Devil and the other God."[50]

In sum, the attempt to create a neutral zone by carving the universe into a trichotomy of values does not avoid the problem of "preferred position" theorizing. On the contrary, both in its descriptions of the categories and in its assignment of controversial instances to those categories, this approach necessarily presupposes a preferred position.

The "Common Denominator" Approach

A related version of neutrality, which might also be regarded as a variation on the secularism theme, regards basic secular values as a kind of "common denominator" on which citizens of differing secular and religious views can unite. These common values provide, in Kent Greenawalt's phrase, a "common currency of political discourse."[51] As long as government acts in pursuit of only these shared values, it can be said to be acting "neutrally." Conversely, if government pursues values that some citizens favor and others reject, it departs from the requirement of neutrality.

David Richards, for example, argues that the state should be neutral in matters of religion and morality.[52] To comply with this requirement of neutrality, "[p]ublic power must be limited to the pursuit of the general goods that rational and reasonable people would want protected, as conditions of whatever else they want."[53] In defining these general goods, Richards invokes Locke's description of "civil interests," which include "'life, liberty, health, and indolency of body; and the possession of outward things, such as money, lands, houses, furniture, and the like.'"[54] He illustrates how confining government to the pursuit of "general goods" would affect religious interests and beliefs:

> The state may, for example, require that babies be washed if washing is understood to secure health interests, but it may not do so if the aim is not such an interest, for example in the case of compulsory baptism. The state may not stop a person from killing a calf in a religious ritual if no civil interest would be secured by such a prohibition, but it may forbid taking the life of a child in such a ritual.[55]

In sum, the state may not promote or oppose religious interests or values except to the extent that these interests or values benefit or suffer indirectly from secular policies. The state may interfere with the exercise of religion when it is acting to further a "general good" but not merely because of disagreement with the religion itself.

This position is held out as neutral, once again, because it limits the state to the pursuit of values or goods that all citizens are thought to accept. The "common denominator" strategy is attractive and, on the surface at least, plausible. It does seem that there are certain values—health, bodily security, economic prosperity, perhaps—that all or nearly all citizens support. Can a government that pursues these and only these commonly held values be regarded as "neutral"?

Upon closer examination, however, the common denominator approach turns out to be based on a misdescription. The approach depicts nonreligious citizens as accepting the proposition that legislation and public policy may properly be based on certain secular considerations. It portrays religious citizens as accepting two severable propositions: (1) that public policy may be based on certain secular considerations and (2) that public policy may also be based on religious considerations (such as biblical precepts or spiritual values). The religious and nonreligious citizens disagree about proposition (2) but agree on proposition (1). Consequently, proposition (1) provides a shared, and hence "neutral," basis for public policy.

But this depiction is inaccurate, because for many religious citizens propositions (1) and (2) are likely not severable. Those citizens may believe that secular considerations are proper and likely to lead to appropriate public policies *if* religious considerations also receive due attention. Conversely, if religious concerns and values are systematically excluded, the monopoly of secular reasons over public discourse might well produce unjust or inappropriate decisions. This kind of religious citizen, in other words, supports not two independent propositions but rather the single, complex proposition that both secular and religious influences must play a part in public policy. (Indeed, this kind of citizen may not even accept the assumption that there is any real and manageable distinction between secular and religious values.) Consequently, there is no unifying proposition that can serve as a common denominator among citizens.[56]

In more familiar contexts, we would immediately spot the common denominator strategy as fraudulent. Suppose Dad and daughter are discussing what to have for dinner. Daughter proposes: "Let's just have dessert." Dad suggests that it would be better to have a full meal, with salad, meat, fruit, vegetables, and *then* dessert. Daughter responds: "Obviously, Dad, we have some disagreements. But there is one thing we agree on; we both want dessert. Clearly, the appropriate solution—the 'neutral' solution—is to accept what we agree on. So serve up the dessert." Dad is not likely to be taken in by this ploy. The supposed agreement is spurious because Dad wants dessert *if and only if* it is preceded by other, more nutritious food.

Or suppose two candidates for high public office are discussing the terms and format of a contemplated television debate. The first candidate, although she agrees that domestic issues should be discussed, also has an impressive record on foreign policy. She argues, therefore, that both foreign and domestic issues should be included in the debate. The second candidate has no experience in foreign policy and would prefer that the debate deal only with domestic issues. Suppose the second candidate proposes that in view of their disagreements, the proper course is to adopt a neutral position and thus to include in the debate only issues that the candidates both agree to include — that is, domestic issues. This claim to neutrality would be transparently bogus.

The effort to depict as "neutral" a restriction limiting government to the pursuit of supposedly shared secular values is similarly misleading.[57] Again, the public schools can serve as an example. There may be "secular" subjects and perspectives that nearly everyone would agree to include in the school curriculum. Some citizens may also believe that certain religious topics or perspectives should be included. Exclusion of those subjects cannot plausibly be characterized as neutral on the ground that these are controversial while the secular subjects are not. Even religious citizens who agree that secular subjects should be included (and for whom the schools' secular teachings do not directly contradict tenets of religious faith) do not thereby approve the secular subjects if they constitute a monopoly within the curriculum. On the contrary, as Michael McConnell has explained:

> If the public school day and all its teaching is strictly secular, the child is likely to learn the lesson that religion is irrelevant to the significant things of this world, or at least that the spiritual realm is radically distinct and separate from the temporal. However unintended, these are lessons about religion. They are not "neutral." Studious silence on a subject that parents may say touches all of life is an eloquent refutation.[58]

There is, consequently, no "common denominator" of shared beliefs and values that can plausibly support a "neutral" approach to religious freedom.

Symbolic Neutrality

The deficiencies in other versions of neutrality may push proponents of this ideal to a desperate expedient. Perhaps we cannot explain what neutrality *is* and thus cannot realistically require government to *be* neutral in matters of religion. But might we not demand that government at least *appear* to be neutral? Might it not be wise, in other words, to suspend any requirement of *actual* neutrality and to substitute instead a requirement of *symbolic* neutrality?

In the last decade or so, the appeal of symbolic neutrality has become conspicuous. Conceding that "[e]stablishment principles are simply not susceptible to consistent interpretation," William Marshall has called for "a jurisprudence that is primarily 'symbolic' and not 'substantive' . . . [and that is thus] concerned less with the substantive goal of limiting certain types of government involvements and supports of religion than with eliminating the *perception* of improper government action."[59] Marshall illustrates the distinction: "[A]ssume a state provides direct financial payment to a minister. The establishment harm is not in the payment. It is in what the payment symbolizes."[60] On the judicial level, the appeal of symbolic neutrality is most evident in the acceptance of the so-called endorsement test proposed by Justice Sandra Day O'Connor in *Lynch v. Donnelly*.[61] A version of that test, which forbids government to adopt laws or engage in practices that are either intended or perceived as expressing approval or disapproval of religion, was embraced by a majority of justices in *American Civil Liberties Union v. Allegheny County*.[62] The test has also won praise from numerous commentators.[63]

As suggested previously, the attraction of this focus on symbolic neutrality reflects the deficiencies in the attempted formulations of actual or substantive neutrality. Perhaps we cannot define just what it would mean for government to *be* neutral, but surely we can at least say when an action *appears to be* neutral. The invitation to adopt the *appearance* of neutrality as the dispositive criterion is seductive because it seemingly requires us only to know our own minds and perceptions.

In this respect, the turn toward symbolic neutrality is reminiscent of philosophical attempts to overcome difficulties in achieving knowledge of the external world by turning inward and adopting human perceptions themselves as the proper objects of immediate knowledge. The "sense datum" approach to knowledge advocated by some philosophers in the first half of this century illustrates the strategy.[64] These philosophers argued that if we focus on perceptual phenomena, we can achieve certainty, at least in some matters.[65] If I say, "A cow is standing by the barn," my assertion may be wrong. The animal standing by the barn may be a horse. Or there may be nothing "out there" at all; I may be hallucinating. But if I say, "I see a brown patch," I cannot be wrong, since I am only making an assertion regarding my own sense perceptions, about which I can hardly be mistaken. [66] At least, so the argument runs.

The turn to symbolic neutrality reflects a similar strategy. If I say that government *is*, or *is not*, acting neutrally, someone may — and usually will — disagree. The ensuing debate is likely to prove embarrassing; it may show that I cannot give a coherent explanation — and certainly not a "neutral" explanation — of what "neutrality" even means. But if I merely say that government *appears* (to me) to be acting neutrally, how can anyone contradict me? Thus, the shift to a doctrine that focuses on the symbolic aspects of governmental action, while eliminating the necessity of defining what neutrality actually is, seems to offer a less vulnerable foundation for us to make assertions and draw conclusions.

Unfortunately, this strategy is deficient in the same way that the sense-datum approach to knowledge has been shown to be deficient. Responding to the contention that sense-datum sentences such as "I see magenta now" are "incorrigible," or incapable of being falsified, J.L. Austin pointed out that such sentences may be false because the speaker may use words incorrectly. "I may say 'Magenta' wrongly," Austin observed, "either by a mere slip, having meant to say 'Vermillion'; or *because I don't know quite what 'magenta' means, what shade of colour is called magenta.*" [67] With respect to sense-datum statements such as "I see magenta," the kind of error identified by Austin may seem to be technically possible but avoidable in practice, and Austin acknowledged as much. We can prevent such mistakes by being sure we know the conventional meaning or usage of "magenta" before we use the word and then by attending carefully to our perceptions.

However, the problem identified by Austin becomes much more persistent when we make assertions that government appears, or does not appear, to be acting neutrally with respect to religion. As Austin's argument makes clear, even statements about how things "appear" presuppose that we understand the accepted or conventional meaning of the words we are using. At most, therefore, statements about appearances might permit us to avoid determining whether our perceptions correspond to some external reality; such statements do nothing to eliminate confusion or conceptual deficiencies that inhere in the words or concepts we use. Hence, if we cannot satisfactorily explain what a position of "neutrality" *is*, we cannot say whether government *appears to be* adhering to such a position.

Consider, for example, the issue in *Everson v. Board of Education*. *Everson* insisted on governmental neutrality in matters of religion, but what would be the neutral course in that case? Does the state act neutrally when it pays to bus children to parochial school? Some of the justices argued that the policy was not neutral because it involved government in religion, gave assistance to religion, and facilitated religious activities.[68] Other justices argued that the state's policy was neutral because it merely put religious-school students on an equal footing with public-school students, whose transportation costs were also paid by the state.[69]

These differing views plainly reflected differing conceptions of neutrality and hence, one may infer, differing background beliefs about religion, government, and the proper relationship between them. The critical question at this point is whether such disagreements might be reconciled, or avoided, by abandoning the question of whether the state's policy *is* neutral and instead asking whether the policy *appears to be* neutral. And the obvious answer is that amending the question to ask about appearances does not even touch the problem; the disagreement remains as lively as ever. If neutrality means noninvolvement or "no aid," as the dissenters believed, then the state policy both *is* and *appears to be* a violation of neutrality. If neutrality means giving religious-school students the same assistance that public-school students receive, as the majority supposed, then the policy *is* and *appears* to be neutral. And if the very notion of neutrality in these matters is disputed or confused, then asking whether the state policy *appears* to be neutral does nothing to resolve the difficulty.[70]

Neutrality as a Matter of Degree?

One objection to the preceding analysis might suggest that the analysis mistakenly treats neutrality as an all-or-nothing matter. To be sure, we might argue, complete or absolute neutrality is unattainable. But surely, it may appear, some governments or positions are "more neutral," or perhaps "closer to being neutral," than others. A proposal for the establishment of interdenominational Christianity is not neutral, but it may seem more neutral than an argument for the establishment of one particular Christian sect; and a position favoring accommodation of "religion" generally — or, even more broadly, of "conscience" — seems more neutral still. Thus, it might be argued that although government can never be fully neutral in matters of religion, the Constitution requires government to be as neutral as it possibly can be.[71]

This is an appealing, and at first glance, a plausible suggestion. If the analysis of this and the preceding chapter is correct, however, then the proposal to treat neutrality as a matter of degree is seriously misleading. Much of the foregoing discussion has tried to show, in essence, that the ideal of religious neutrality is simply not coherent. And if the ideal of neutrality is not coherent, then it makes no sense to urge government to be "as neutral as possible." As an illustration, suppose that a teacher tells a student to draw a straight line, and the student says, "I can't seem to do it." The teacher might sensibly respond, "I know you can't draw a *perfectly* straight line, but draw as straight a line as possible." But if the teacher says to draw a square circle and the student says, "It can't be done," it would be quite senseless for the teacher to answer, "I know you can't do it perfectly, but draw as square a circle as possible."

In a similar way, the foregoing analysis suggests that at bottom, religious neutrality is not a coherent ideal. The notion of neutrality holds that government should be impartial toward, and should treat equally, all religious beliefs, neither privileging nor disfavoring any set of beliefs. Consequently, the demand for neutrality calls for the relationship between government and religion to be determined without privileging or adopting any of the competing religious and secular positions within the culture. But this aspiration is not merely unrealistic or difficult to attain *in practice*; upon reflection, the aspiration is scarcely intelligible. How *could* a regime or theory regulating the relations between government and religion be elaborated and defended except on the basis of the beliefs and values of one or more of the competing religious and secular positions within the culture?

Still, it at least *seems* plausible to say that some positions are "more neutral" than others. This appearance, however, may be deceitful; it may reflect, implicitly but inevitably, a tacit assumption that some persons, groups, or belief systems "count," or are entitled to full consideration and equal treatment by the state, and that other persons, groups, or belief systems do not "count" in this sense.

As an illustration, imagine a society (much like colonial America) in which nearly everyone is a Protestant of one denomination or another, while Catholics, Jews, Muslims, and other kinds of believers are few and, as far as the mainstream society is concerned, almost invisible. In this kind of society, no one would think to describe a proposal favoring one Protestant sect over the others as "neutral." But it might seem quite natural — for Protestants, at least — to describe as religiously "neutral" a proposal benefiting all

Protestant denominations and founded in assumptions common to Protestantism generally. The proposal treats equally all the groups that figure in the prevalent understanding of groups that must be taken account of.

In this vein, proponents of a "no preference" version of religious freedom still sometimes characterize as nonpreferential or nondiscriminatory programs that benefited or subsidized Christianity generally but not other religions during the founding era.[72] These characterizations benignly neglect to notice that there were also Jews living in the country at that time.[73] The Jews, it seems, somehow disappear from view in such descriptions; they do not "count."

Suppose now that someone points out this omission. Someone points out, in other words, that although a particular measure is compatible with and beneficial to the various groups of Protestants, it implicitly rejects the beliefs and slights the interests of a perhaps inconspicuous but nonetheless real minority — Catholics, Jews, Muslims, and others. How could proponents of the measure respond? They might simply drop the rhetoric of "neutrality" and defend the measure on straightforward majoritarian grounds. But this defense would encounter the common objections that majority rule should not be unlimited and that religious freedom especially should not be limited even to satisfy the desires of a powerful majority.[74]

For these and other reasons, proponents of the measure might decline to defend it in starkly majoritarian terms or to relinquish the appealing rhetoric of neutrality. So they might argue that their position, though not completely or absolutely neutral, still is "approximately neutral" or at least that it is "more neutral" than its alternatives. But now it is unclear what this description could mean. In what sense is the "general Protestantism" measure even approximately "neutral"?

One possibility is that the description is nothing more than a deceptive way of saying that the broader measure is consistent with the beliefs and interests of a majority (perhaps a large majority). Saying that a measure is "approximately neutral," or "neutral" though not absolutely so, would merely be a way of saying that it is not offensive to *most citizens. That* claim could be more candidly presented, however, in straightforward numerical or majoritarian terms. (And some claims commonly made by courts and scholars in the language of neutrality would, if translated into numerical terms, likely prove false as an empirical matter.)

Or perhaps the language of "more neutral" or "almost neutral" implies something more. That language does seem to serve, after all, to distinguish the measure benefiting Protestantism generally from a measure benefiting a particular Protestant sect — and not only, arguably, on numerical grounds. Among Protestants, rather, the broader measure may seem neutral because it does not favor *any* version of Protestantism over any other.

That difference is important *to Protestants*. It is less important, presumably, to non-Protestants; *their* interests are neglected by measures favoring either a single Protestant sect or Protestantism generally. If the broader measure is approved on the ground that it is "more neutral," therefore, the clear message is that a measure's acceptability will be determined by how it affects Protestants; validity will be determined in accordance with a criterion that has meaning for Protestants but not for non-Protestants. By this standard, if a measure is not neutral among Protestants, it will be unacceptable; if a measure is neutral among Protestants but not toward others, the measure will be approved. In this way, the language of "more neutral" plainly suggests that non-Protestants do not count, or at least do not count for as much as other groups whom the law must treat equally or with "neutrality."

The point can be put differently: If the language of "neutrality" seems to add something to the more quantitative language of majority or supermajority support, that is because *within the universe of Protestants*, a measure benefiting Protestantism in general *is*, in an intuitively understandable sense, "neutral." But the corollary connotation of such language is that non-Protestants are not — not fully, at least — part of the relevant social and political universe. They do not count. [75]

In sum, the language of "more neutral," or of "approximate neutrality," is either a deceptive way of presenting simple majoritarianism, with all the familiar advantages and objections that attend majoritarianism in this area, or else it pretends to honor a commitment to treat all citizens equally by quietly pushing those who are *not* treated equally out of the picture. [76] But this sort of marginalization or exclusion, ironically, seems the most extreme kind of departure from the value of equality that claims of religious neutrality seek to honor. [77]

The Failure of the Quest for Neutrality

The foregoing discussion suggests that the quest for neutrality, despite its understandable appeal and the tenacity with which it has been pursued, is an attempt to grasp an illusion. Upon reflection, this failure should not be surprising. The impossibility of a truly "neutral" theory of religious freedom is analogous to the impossibility, recognized by modern philosophers, of finding some outside Archimedean point[78]—or, as it is sometimes said, a "God's Eye View"[79]—from which to look down on and describe reality. Descriptions of reality are always undertaken from a point within reality. In the same way, theories of religious freedom are always offered from the viewpoint of one of the competing positions that generate the need for such a theory; there is no neutral vantage point that can permit the theorist or judge to transcend these competing positions. Hence, insofar as a genuine and satisfactory theory of religious freedom would need to be "neutral" in this sense, rather than one that privileges one of the competing positions from the outset, a theory of religious freedom is as illusory as the ideal of neutrality it seeks to embody.

8

A Secular Theory
of Religious Freedom?

A possible response to the preceding discussion would be to concede the basic point and then simply forge ahead. Perhaps the attempt to equate secularism with neutrality *is* implausible, and "preferred position" theorizing is the only kind of theorizing there is. Why not just drop the pretense of neutrality, openly proclaim that the preferred position is a secular one, and then proceed to construct a theory of religious freedom on the basis of avowedly secular premises?[1] The theory could be neutrally *applied*, perhaps; if it is not neutral in its selection of background beliefs or premises, it could hardly be condemned for that reason, since neutrality at that level is impossible in any event.

The foregoing chapters already suggest threshold objections to this proposal. First, an openly nonneutral theory is not what judges and legal scholars have aspired to provide. More important, there is good reason for their loftier aspirations: As discussed in chapter 6, even if a theory can be constructed on the basis of nonneutral secular premises (or, for that matter, nonneutral religious premises), it is doubtful whether this could aptly be described as a theory of "religious freedom."

In addition, supposing that the development of a "preferred position" theory is attractive, why should the preferred position be a purely secular one? It is no answer to say that the Constitution requires government to be secular: What (if anything) the Constitution requires of government with respect to religion is, after all, precisely the question at issue. Neither is it plausible to say that a secular position is appropriate because that position is most consistent with the beliefs and values of the American people. Although some legal academics are fond of saying that ours is a secular republic, or that the Constitution created a secular republic,[2] this seems to be an instance of wishful thinking or of hoping that saying something often enough will make it so. In fact, both the "secular republic" and "religious people" or "Christian nation" themes have enjoyed, and continue to enjoy, considerable support in American discourse — which suggests that neither theme by itself is adequate to the reality. As Martin Marty observes, ours is a "religio-secular, operative-passional, sacro-secular life and society."[3] Thus, the privileging of a purely secular position would do violence to the complexity of both our history and our contemporary culture.[4]

Although I believe these to be telling and perhaps decisive objections to any proposal for constructing a wholly secular theory of religious freedom, I intend in this chapter to set them aside in order to pursue a different question: Even if we agree to assume a secular perspective, or to start from secular premises, can we construct an adequate theory of religious freedom? Secular values, to be sure, can in some contexts support policies of religious freedom. A completely agnostic ruler might find good secular reasons for permitting subjects to hold and live in accordance with some religious beliefs, even though the ruler regards those beliefs as rank superstition. But it does not follow from the fact that secular rationales may in some contexts support *religious freedom* that they can also generate a plausible *principle* or *theory* of religious freedom. Whether, how, and to what extent religious freedom should be respected might depend on a context-specific balancing of competing interests, and that balancing might not be reducible to any consistent theory or general principle — except of course, for the "principle" of doing whatever is best under the circumstances. Secular rationales, in short, might leave the matter of religious freedom squarely within the realm of prudentialism.

I will argue in this chapter that this is, in fact, the case. The same secular rationale may in some contexts suggest that religious belief and practice be permitted or accommodated while supporting just the opposite conclusion in a different context. And there is no reason to suppose that the variety of contextual and prudential judgments can somehow be plausibly united under any general theory.[5]

I cannot, of course, consider every possible secular rationale for religious freedom. Instead, the discussion will focus on what may be the three most common and influential rationales. The first of these, which we may call the "civic virtue rationale," was familiar at the time of the American founding, and it remains important today. The second consideration may be called the "civil peace rationale"; it has also been important throughout this nation's history. The third, or "nonalienation rationale," is of more recent vintage, but in the last decade it has achieved considerable prominence. Any of these rationales *may* support policies of religious freedom in some circumstances, but none, I will argue, can plausibly support any general or consistent policy that might be embodied in a principle or theory.[6]

The Civic Virtue Rationale

The civic virtue rationale asserts, in essence, that religious freedom is important because religion is an especially important source of the qualities that must be inculcated in citizens if the social order is to prosper. This view of religion was common at the time of the founding.[7] The civic virtue rationale is also offered in contemporary legal scholarship as a justification for religious freedom.[8]

It is helpful to break this argument down into two claims. The rationale asserts, first, that religion is necessary to a society because it is an especially important source of civic virtue. Second, the rationale claims that the best way for government to ensure the continuing vitality of religion in society is to adopt some particular version of religious freedom, such as the principle requiring "strict separation" between government and religion. Both of these claims *may* be true in some contexts. But neither can be taken as true, I will argue, in any general or universal way.

Religion as a Source of Civic Virtue

The notion that religion is an essential source of civic virtue is an old one in this country. Tocqueville reported:

> I do not know whether all Americans have a sincere faith in their religion — for who can search the human heart? — but I am certain that they hold it indispensable to the maintenance of republican institutions. This opinion is not peculiar to a class of citizens, but it belongs to the whole nation and to every rank of society.[9]

Competing with this commendatory view of religion, however, is an equally venerable but directly contrary argument, which asserts that religion breeds pernicious qualities in citizens. An older version of this theme emphasized that religion — Christianity in particular — produces otherworldliness and hence a lack of civic commitment. In this way, Edward Gibbon linked Christianity and its cultivation of otherworldliness to the decline of the Roman Empire. [10]

In a more common post-Enlightenment variant, critics contend that religion fosters intolerance and authoritarianism. Steven Gey's criticism is characteristic; Gey argues that "the very structure of religious ideas and practice are contrary to the mode of thought necessary to foster democratic self-governance" and that "the authoritarian and undemocratic nature of religion is inconsistent with the anti-authoritarian and democratic biases of the Constitution." [11] Michael Smith discerns this kind of negative assessment of religion in the thinking of some Supreme Court justices. [12]

How would one decide between these favorable and unfavorable depictions of religion? Are the social fruits of religion sweet or bitter? Upon reflection it should be plain, I think, that these questions are not susceptible of any general or uniform response. The only plausible answer, rather, is "It depends" — on the kind of religion, the kind of society, and the existence and effectiveness of other institutions for inculcating civic virtue.

In the first place, we cannot sensibly talk about the effects of "religion" on character because different forms of religion attempt to inculcate very different character traits. [13] Quakers do not teach the same moral values that Muslims teach; fundamentalist Christians do not favor the same personal characteristics that Unitarians value. These differences in beliefs and values implicate, sometimes explicitly and directly, the question of the proper relationship between the believer and the human law. Jehovah's Witnesses have famously refused to salute the flag because, perhaps among other reasons, they regard it as an image subject to the biblical prohibition against the worship of graven images. [14] Conversely, Mormons are taught to be "subject to kings, presidents, rulers, and magistrates, and [to] obey[ ], honor[ ], and sustain[ ] the law." [15] Of course, even these assertions greatly oversimplify by implying that Muslims, or fundamentalist Christians, or Mormons constitute monistic communities uniformly committed to a single set of values or character traits.

Whether religion is conducive to civic virtue also depends on the kind of virtues that a particular society chooses to foster. Suppose, for example, that a given religion teaches its adherents, as Gibbon believed Christianity did, to be acquiescent and detached from worldly concerns because the affairs of this world are of little moment compared to the interests of eternity. These teachings might be nicely compatible with a society or political community that desires docile, peaceable citizens. The same teachings would perhaps be antithetical to the values of a different kind of community — a Spartan regime, for example, or a "republican" community that regards active citizen participation in public life as the essential mark of a healthy society. Of course, the values and character traits favored by any particular actual community are likely to be complex, controversial, and changeable (as the liberalism/civic republicanism debate of recent years reflects), so that even if it were possible to say that "religion" in general inculcates a given set of character traits, it might still be difficult to say that these traits either simply are or simply are not conducive to the flourishing of that community.

The matter is even more complex because of the difficulty of characterizing values or personality traits. Consider for example Steven Gey's assertion that religion instills "authoritarian" qualities antithetical to our democratic community. It is true that a democracy is unlikely to prize authoritarian qualities when they are labeled as such. But a democratic community might very well want citizens who are "orderly," or who exhibit a proper respect for law. Thus, even if Gey were correct that "religion" promotes qualities that critics will want to describe as authoritarian, his position would still be little more than an oversimplification hiding behind a pejorative label.

Finally, the importance of religion in inculcating civic virtue depends on whether and to what extent other institutions are capable of performing that task. Mark Tushnet observes that "[r]eligion may be one among several methods of inculcating civic virtue, rather than a necessary method."[16] Other institutions — most obviously families and schools but also associations such as civic and political organizations, scouting programs, service clubs, and athletic leagues — conceivably might make religion an inessential contributor to the moral formation of citizens' character.

These observations are not intended to show that religion is in fact socially dispensable or that the assertion of a relationship between religion and civic virtue is simply false. The point, rather, is that generalizations in this area are difficult. Whether a society depends on religion for forming the moral character of its citizens will depend on a host of variable circumstances. Consequently, the civic virtue claim provides a shaky basis for constructing a general theory of religious freedom.

Why (and What Kind of) Religious Freedom?

Suppose, however, that the foregoing objections to the civic virtue rationale are all unpersuasive or that they are somehow overcome. In other words, suppose it is established that "religion," in some generic sense, is an essential foundation for civic virtue. From this it seems to follow that *religion* is important to social flourishing. But does anything follow with respect to *religious freedom*?

It should be sobering at this point to recall that in times past a civic virtue rationale was commonly invoked *not* to support what we would call *religious freedom*, but rather to support *religious establishment*.[17] The Massachusetts Constitution of 1780 justified compulsory worship and the public subsidization of religion on the premise that "the happiness of a people, and the good order and preservation of civil government, essentially depend upon piety, religion, and morality."[18] Similarly, the Virginia assessments bill that Jefferson and Madison successfully opposed justified public support for religion on the ground that "the general diffusion of Christian knowledge hath a natural tendency to correct the morals of men, restrain their vices, and preserve the peace of society."[19] In short, early proponents of the civic virtue rationale used it to argue for a conclusion just opposite that typically favored by current proponents. Religion is essential for the inculcation of civic virtue, it was argued, and therefore government ought to support religion in various ways, many of which involved the use of coercion.

If anything, the logic of the earlier proponents seems more natural and plausible than the currently popular view. If a particular institution is essential to society, it seems to follow that government should use its powers to foster or promote that institution, instead of simply leaving the institution to fend for itself (much less excluding it from benefits, such as public subsidies, for which other institutions *are* eligible).[20] Our public education system is founded on the premise that because an educated citizenry is necessary to society, it is appropriate for the state to compel citizens to spend ten or more years of their lives in school. Indeed, a major purpose of compulsory education is precisely to inculcate civic virtue in young citizens.[21] In this area, therefore, something like the civic virtue rationale is still used to justify compulsion, not freedom from compulsion. The rationale might well be used in the same way to support governmental promotion of religion.

However, the civic virtue rationale for compulsion, like the civic virtue rationale for freedom, is subject to objections. It has often been suggested that religion in this country is stronger than in other countries precisely because it does *not* receive governmental encouragement or support. [22] This contention might seem paradoxical. Why would precluding one kind of institution from receiving, for example, governmental subsidies for which other institutions are eligible strengthen rather than weaken the excluded institution?

Probably the most common answer, elaborated long ago by Tocqueville, asserts that religion loses popular appeal by being associated with governments that themselves seem oppressive or illegitimate. "[W]hen religion clings to the interests of the world," Tocqueville explained, "it becomes almost as fragile a thing as the powers of earth. . . . [I]f it be connected with their ephemeral power, it shares their fortunes and may fall with those transient passions which alone supported them." [23] The American clergy had perceived this truth and hence had preserved their position. [24] In Europe, conversely, "Christianity has been intimately united to the powers of the earth. Those powers are now in decay, and it is, as it were, buried under their ruins." [25]

This explanation seems plausible enough, but it also suggests the contextual nature of the relationship between governmental support and religious vitality. If religion receives support from and hence is associated with an *unpopular* or oppressive government, then religion might naturally lose credibility. This may well have been true, as Tocqueville argued, for churches associated with monarchical regimes that were perceived as undemocratic and oppressive. Similarly, Tocqueville observed that association with government is particularly perilous to religion in times of political turbulence and upheaval. [26] Conversely, if a government is stable and enjoys prestige or respect among the citizenry, then religion might naturally benefit by association with government. That at least seems to be the assumption in modern decisions that condemn the "symbolic union" of church and state; the decisions assume that religions favored by this union will be improperly strengthened, not weakened. [27]

Whether a policy of "no aid" or "strict separation" will strengthen religion also depends on the overall role of government in the community. If government generally maintains a minimalist or lais-

sez-faire position with respect to society, religion will seemingly be
at no relative disadvantage if it receives no special governmental
assistance. Indeed, for government to single out religion for special
benefits or subsidies might understandably provoke jealousy and
resentment, thereby weakening religion over the long run. Conversely, if government taxes citizens heavily in order to promote or
subsidize a wide range of interests and projects, a policy of excluding
religion from such general benefits might well undermine religion. [28]
Michael Paulsen suggests that "the most effective way for the modern state to disparage any institution is to deny it financial benefits
to which others are entitled." [29] For example, if government subsi-
dizes all schools in the community *except* for religious schools, the
religious schools seem to be at a clear disadvantage. [30]

The basic point, once again, is not that the civic virtue rationale
is false. Both of its claims are almost surely true in some contexts.
At some times and in some societies, religion may be a valuable or
even indispensable source of civic virtue. And in some situations,
the best way for government to ensure the vitality of religion may
be to leave religion strictly alone. [31] In other situations, these conditions may not obtain. Consequently, the civic virtue rationale may
in some contexts provide a cogent argument for particular positions
that we would associate with "religious freedom," but that rationale
does not offer a firm foundation on which to build a general *principle*
or *theory* of religious freedom.

The Civil Peace Rationale

Like the civic virtue rationale, the civil peace rationale can be presented in the form of two claims. First, religion is an especially
powerful source of civil strife. Second, the best way to contain the
volatile potential of religion is for government to adopt some particular version of religious freedom, such as the version that insists on
a "strict separation" between church and state.

For present purposes, I do not want to challenge the first of
these claims. The wars of religion in Europe and the present exam-
ples of, say, Ireland or India support the belief that religion *can be* a
source of serious civil strife. Critics of this rationale sometimes point
out that in this country nonreligious issues — slavery, unionization,
racial desegregation, the Vietnam war — have been far more divisive
than religion per se has been. [32] But it might be that religion has
been less divisive in this country precisely because we have generally

adhered to sound policies of religious freedom.[33] Or a proponent of the civil peace rationale might argue that religion is always a *potentially* explosive matter and that a constitutional principle should be crafted so as to avoid this danger even when it is not imminent. For now it is enough to say that in these inherently speculative matters it is hard to show that the first claim made in the civil peace rationale is flatly *false*, and for purposes of argument we may therefore provisionally accept it as true.

The difficulty arises with the second claim, which asserts that the best way to avoid civil strife is for government to adopt some particular version of religious freedom, such as the "strict separation" version. Again, the prevailing view for centuries held exactly to the contrary: Social peace and stability are best promoted if the state adopts and supports an official religion and discourages or suppresses deviations from that religion.[34] As between these antithetical views of the relationship between religious freedom and civil peace, it seems implausible to suppose that either view is simply and always right while the other is simply and always wrong. The policy best calculated to promote civil peace, rather, will depend on a variety of circumstances.

In a community that exhibits significant religious diversity, for example, it may be that no particular religion has any realistic chance of dominating the government. A nonestablishment policy may thus be acceptable, at least as a sort of "second best" arrangement, to all concerned, and it might reduce any temptation to compete for official recognition.[35] Conversely, in a community where most citizens adhere to a common religion, new issues arise. If religious minorities are economically or militarily powerful, nonestablishment might still be the policy best calculated to promote civil peace. But if a minority is small and powerless and if its beliefs and practices are highly offensive to the dominant group, suppression of the minority might be the more stabilizing course. As Peter Nicholson points out: "[I]f one could eliminate the objectionable religion . . . without the undesirable side-effects, then one would stamp them out. Likewise, one would not have to tolerate the opinions and actions of any minority which was sufficiently easily identified, small, economically inessential and powerless."[36]

The degree of pluralism is not the only factor that helps to determine which course will promote greater stability. The specific content of religious beliefs and the intensity with which they are held are also relevant concerns. A believer whose faith is either lukewarm or latitudinarian or both may have no difficulty associating closely with persons of different faiths. Indeed, a believer might even find spiritual value in living amid a plurality of religious beliefs.[37] Conversely, a more fervent and dogmatic faith may find such a situation unacceptable. Steven Runciman has observed:

> A broad-minded view of the private belief of others undoubtedly makes for the happiness of society; but it is an attitude impossible for those whose personal religion is strong. For if we know that we have found the key and guiding principle of Life, we cannot allow our friends to flounder blindly in the darkness. . . . Opinions may vary as to the nature of the help that should be given, whether peaceful persuasion and a shining example, or the sword and the *auto-da-fé*. But no really religious man can pass the unbeliever by and do nothing.[38]

In short, the traditional view that an established religion promotes civil stability is probably correct for some circumstances; the modern notion that nonestablishment reduces civil strife is true for other settings. As Michael Sandel points out: "Under present conditions, such calculations [about how to avoid civil strife] may or may not support the separation of church and state. . . . [A] strict separation of church and state may at times provoke more strife than it prevents."[39]

Even this ambivalent conclusion greatly oversimplifies the matter, however, because issues of religious freedom almost never involve an either/or choice for or against "separation of church and state." As modern controversies reflect, the real questions concern a complex range of regulations or measures of assistance that affect a diverse assortment of religious beliefs and practices in different ways. To be sure, one can be relentlessly reductionist and group a whole array of thematically related measures — daily *mandatory* school prayer, daily oral but *nonmandatory* school prayer, a daily "moment of silence," occasional prayers at special school ceremonies such as graduation exercises, occasional prayers at extracurricular events such as football games — under the general heading of "school prayer," or under the even more general heading of "religious establishment," and then uphold or reject them as a lump. But if the concern is to minimize civil strife, that all-or-nothing course would seem ill-advised. Forbidding a particular measure *might* promote civil peace, or it might generate more strife than it quells, and there is no reason to suppose that the same answer will obtain for all of these thematically related but nonetheless different measures.

The important point here is that the strife-minimizing course is likely to vary from time to time and place to place. It may be that in an extremely homogenous community, few if any students would object to school prayer, and prohibiting the practice might cause considerable dissatisfaction.[40] Conversely, in a radically pluralistic school district in which many students are agnostic, the opposite course might be indicated. And most communities will likely fall in between these extremes. Hence, deciding how to reduce civil strife would require a careful and context-sensitive judgment that would consider both the nature of the community and the specific nature of the measure at issue.

In short, if the government's goal is to reduce civil strife, there is no general formula that can tell it how to achieve this objective. The matter calls, rather, for a prudential judgment. And that sort of judgment cannot readily be domesticated under the heading of a "principle" or "theory" of religious freedom.

The Nonalienation Rationale

By contrast to the two rationales already discussed, both of which have a long history in this country, the prominence of the nonalienation rationale is more recent; it has been developed over the last decade, largely in connection with a position that understands the establishment clause as a prohibition against governmental messages that endorse or disapprove of religion.[41] The nonalienation rationale closely parallels the civil peace rationale — except that the feared evil has been scaled down. Whereas the older rationale suggested a danger of serious social disruption perhaps leading to political disintegration,[42] the newer rationale envisions and seeks to avoid a more quiet withdrawal of some citizens from the political community because of their sense of second-class status.[43]

Just as the civil peace rationale was presented in the form of two claims, the nonalienation rationale can be understood in terms of two parallel claims. The first claim asserts that religion is an especially potent factor that may cause citizens to become alienated or disaffected from the political community. The second claim contends that the best way to avoid or reduce such citizen alienation is for government to adopt some particular version of religious freedom calculated to promote inclusiveness, such as the "no endorsement" principle.

The first of these claims is surely debatable. Although governmental involvement in or endorsement of religion undoubtedly may alienate or offend some citizens, governmental involvement in any area of life or endorsement of any belief may have the same consequence. Government endorses free enterprise but not socialism, war against North Vietnam or Panama or Iraq rather than nonmilitary sanctions or pacifism, policies of natural-resource development over certain kinds of environmental policies. Any of these messages may offend some citizens and cause them to feel like "outsiders," and it is not clear that governmental endorsement or disapproval of religion produces more alienation than other controversial messages that government may send.[44]

Still, alienation arising from religious or antireligious governmental messages might be more severe than alienation brought about by other controversial governmental actions or messages.[45] And even if religious alienation is not more severe, a proponent of this rationale might argue that it nonetheless ought to be minimized as much as possible. At least for purposes of argument, therefore, we may concede the first claim.

Even so, the second claim cannot be accepted in any general way. To be sure, there may be a connection between some version of religious freedom and the good or value of nonalienation. The problem is that the connection is not a necessary or uniform one, but instead is contingent on shifting and elusive cultural circumstances. Given the religious and secular diversity that exists in this country, *any* resolution of most controversial issues is likely to produce alienation. Consequently, the nonalienation rationale, while it identifies a sensible desideratum for wise political policy, provides an infirm foundation for a general theory or principle of religious freedom.

The point can be illustrated by imagining a hypothetical political community in which devotees of one religion — call them "Baal-worshipers" — constitute 90 percent of the population; the other 10 percent are "Diana-worshipers." The Baal-worshipers tolerate the religion of Diana in the limited sense that they have not made practicing that religion a criminal offense. But they also believe that Diana-worship is evil and offensive and that they would be contaminated by close contact with the disciples of Diana. Or perhaps they believe that Baal would frown on any government that afforded infidels equal political status with Baal's own disciples. Consequently, the community's constitution excludes Diana-worshipers from serving in public office. In short, the constitution is similar in this respect to the constitutions of many American states, both before and for decades after the adoption of the First Amendment, that used religious-oath requirements to exclude, variously, nontheists, non-Christians, or sometimes non-Protestants, from public office.

In this situation, would the adoption of a policy forbidding government to do anything that sends a message endorsing the Baal religion or disapproving the Diana religion reduce citizen alienation? One obvious consequence of such a position is that prohibitions excluding Diana-worshipers from serving in public office would have to be eliminated, since these prohibitions surely send a message disapproving of the Diana religion. This change would probably help to assuage the severe sense of alienation that Diana-worshipers no doubt experience in this Baal-dominated society. But if the result of admitting the Diana-worshipers to equal status is that Baal-worshipers, fearing spiritual contamination, feel compelled to withdraw from public life, then the overall degree of alienation—that is, of a sense of exclusion from political participation on religious grounds—might well increase. Whereas before 10 percent of the population was excluded from participating in government on religious grounds, now 90 percent of the population is precluded from participation on such grounds.

This conclusion does not mean, of course, that the Baal-inspired exclusionary measures are admirable or desirable—only that abandoning them is likely to increase, not reduce, overall citizen alienation. Nor can this conclusion be avoided by the tempting contention that if the exclusionary measures are eliminated, it is not *the government* that is the cause of the Baal-worshipers' alienation but rather the Baal-worshipers themselves. In this situation, as in others, alienation in fact results from a combination of governmental policy and conflicting religious beliefs, and it would merely be misleading to point to either of these factors as *the* cause of alienation. Hence, if government adopts a policy of inclusiveness and nonendorsement, it undeniably has rejected the religious belief which holds that Baal should be recognized and that Diana-worshipers should be excluded. It is true, of course, that if Baal-worshipers did not hold this unfortunate belief they would have no reason to feel alienated. But then the Baal-worshipers could have said the same thing all along to the Diana-worshipers. The statement is formally correct in both cases; indeed, it will always be formally correct to say that those who feel alienated on religious grounds would not need to feel alienated if they did not believe as they do.

Similarly, if we assume (implausibly) that religious beliefs are freely chosen, then we can always say that an alienated group has itself—its own choice of beliefs—to blame for its sense of exclusion.

But if the goal is to reduce overall alienation, these observations are beside the point. The bottom line is that we cannot rely on the desirability of reducing actual alienation as the justification for a position of nonendorsement, because in this context a nonendorsement version of religious freedom will in fact increase overall alienation.

Under other circumstances, of course, this version of religious freedom probably *would* reduce net alienation. If the percentage of Diana-worshipers grows or if many Baal-worshipers lose their sense that association with Diana-worshipers leads to spiritual contamination, then the balance may shift in favor of nonendorsement. In our own society, likewise, there are certain aspects of religious freedom that almost certainly produce a net gain in political inclusion. For example, one could confidently suppose that in this country the absence of an established church avoids more alienation than it produces,[46] even though a few citizens who favor an established church may feel alienated by nonestablishment.[47] On many other issues, however, including school prayer, aid to parochial schools, religious symbols in public displays, and virtually any other issue that excites genuine controversy, the balance of alienation is much harder to assess.[48]

The problem is especially complex because there is no assurance that the balance of alienation, even with respect to a given issue, will be uniform through space and time. In a largely secular community or a politically and religiously liberal community, for example, a "balanced treatment" statute requiring that creationism receive equal time with evolution in the public school curriculum might provoke more disaffection that it would relieve.[49] Hardly anyone in this kind of community, we may suppose, is alienated by the teaching of evolution anyway; but many students and their parents likely *would* be offended by the teaching of what they would regard as fundamentalist religion masquerading as science. Conversely, in a community composed largely of religious conservatives, a "balanced treatment" statute may have just the opposite effect: It may alleviate the considerable alienation generated by the exclusive teaching of what they view as an antireligious doctrine.[50]

Just as the relative offensiveness of particular messages for different groups might vary from community to community, the phenomenon might also change over time. The scholarly treatment of publicly sponsored nativity scenes illustrates this possibility. In 1964, Wilbur Katz suggested that such displays were in principle unconstitutional but might be excused under a *de minimis* rationale.

"If this means that our neutrality is a bit more neutral toward some than toward others," Katz calmly observed, "a sense of humor should enable all of us to accept the situation."[51] By contrast, two decades later, when the Supreme Court approved such a display in *Lynch v. Donnelly*,[52] legal scholars no longer exhibited Katz's sense of humor; they were, rather, incensed.[53] Leo Pfeffer went so far as to compare *Lynch* to the *Dred Scott* decision.[54]

These drastically different reactions were no doubt influenced in part by expectations arising from two decades of secularly inclined constitutional decisions. That likelihood reflects a further difficulty in embodying an effective nonalienation doctrine in constitutional theory and law: Even if an adopted constitutional principle or theory were initially accurate in estimating the relative balance of alienation, the very acceptance of the principle or theory would likely alter the cultural dynamic in which that balance is grounded. Indeed, a principle or theory that purports to forbid all governmental endorsement or disapproval of religion may give rise to a sort of revolution of rising expectations, so that people become more sensitive to, and alienated by, what they formerly accepted with a shrug or perhaps failed even to notice.[55]

Proliferating litigation in recent years over public religious symbols may be an instance of just this sort of revolution. William Marshall, a supporter of the "no endorsement" position, observes and laments this pattern of escalation (although it does not lead him to doubt the wisdom of the "no endorsement" test):

> An unfortunate pattern of litigation has engulfed the religion clause debate. Divergent and often opposing groups seem intent on prohibiting what they deem offensive and have selected the religion clauses as their weapon of choice. Lawsuits attacking "humanist" textbooks, Christmas carols, football game invocations, graduation convocations, nativity scenes and the National Endowment for the Art are just a few of the lawsuits that have been brought by credible organizations.[56]

Nor is there any reason to assume that the escalation is finished. In fact, scholars have suggested, plausibly enough, that the recently adopted "no endorsement" construction of religious freedom ought logically to invalidate numerous other expressions and practices that the Supreme Court has not previously been forced to rule on, including not only the most obvious candidates—for example, the national motto "In God We Trust" and the reference in the Pledge of Allegiance to "one nation under God"—but also the names of cities like Corpus Christi and Los Angeles.[57] It would hardly be surprising if these scholarly suggestions lead to further litigation—and, inevitably, to further disappointment, frustration, and alienation on the part of one group or another.

Faced with this complexity, an advocate of the nonalienation rationale might be tempted to simplify the problem by focusing on only one side of the balance of alienation while ignoring the other side. In this way, he might try to create the appearance of a necessary or uniform relationship—that is, a relationship not closely dependent on cultural context—between political inclusiveness and a version of religious freedom. This is in essence what the Supreme Court has done in its decisions applying the "no endorsement" interpretation of the establishment clause.[58] Those decisions exhibit a simpleminded logic: Religious symbols or messages emanating from government alienate some citizens; therefore, elimination of such symbols and messages will reduce alienation. The Court simply takes no account of the other side of the balance—of the alienation, that is, that many persons feel toward a government that they perceive as indifferent or hostile to religion, and that is likely to be aggravated by the results of the "no endorsement" version of religious freedom.[59] This one-sided approach makes it impossible for the Court to assess whether its decisions do anything to reduce overall alienation, just as it would be impossible to determine whether a business had made a profit if its accountants reported only gross revenues while refusing to acknowledge the business's expenses.

Commentators who support the Court's general approach in this area are often more astute, or at least more candid, in recognizing its limitations. Although they acknowledge that any governmental action is likely to produce alienation in some citizens as it reduces alienation in others, these scholars nonetheless favor a constitutional interpretation requiring government to act in the way that will *minimize* political alienation.[60] Unfortunately, these scholars offer no practical way of measuring net alienation. They may propose simple heuristic formulas, but these formulas are so vague as to be almost useless.

For example, Daniel Conkle advocates an approach that would invalidate governmental messages disapproving of the religious beliefs of "outsiders," but would not be "overly concerned" with messages that offend the religious beliefs of "insiders."[61] However, even assuming that this test would produce net gains in nonalienation if it could be accurately applied,[62] how are we to decide who counts as an "insider" and who qualifies as an "outsider"? Conkle offers little guidance except to suggest that insiders are "those who are part of America's religious mainstream" and that outsiders include "individuals who hold minority religious or irreligious views."[63] But these categories are highly elastic and manipulable. If one frames a category broadly — "Christian," for example, or "theist" — then nearly all American citizens will be "insiders"; if one defines categories more specifically — by denomination, for instance — then everyone will be part of a religious minority. What about fundamentalist Christians, for example? They clearly see themselves as outsiders,[64] but because they are Christians, they might also be regarded as insiders.[65] It is ironic, moreover, that the effort to classify different groups of believers and nonbelievers as "insiders" and "outsiders" for constitutional purposes would seem to ratify and, if it were systematically implemented, even codify the very sense of first-class and second-class status that the nonalienation rationale is ostensibly seeking to overcome.

If scholars favoring the "no endorsement" test cannot present workable methods for measuring net alienation, that failure is hardly surprising. In fact, the task of measuring alienation is a formidable one; in view of the shifting and closely contextual nature of the problem, it seems unlikely that any *general* rule of thumb will perform the task with even approximate accuracy.[66] In the end, therefore, the recommendation that government follow the "least alienating alternative" is closely akin to prescriptions urging government to "promote the general welfare" or to do what is best for the most citizens. Such counsels may be sensible enough, but they are not the kind of counsel that can be usefully embodied in general theories or principles that could be applied in across-the-board fashion.[67] Thus, the nonalienation rationale, even if we accept the value or good it invokes, does not persuasively support a viable theory or principle of religious freedom.

Constitutional Principle and the Political Community

Discussions of constitutional theories often exhibit, not surprisingly, a theoretical quality. The foregoing discussion has sometimes been abstract, and it has enlisted the aid of hypothetical communities and hypothetical religions to support its analysis. Lest it seem that the analysis is relevant only in a hypothetical world, it may be helpful to reflect briefly on how the modern project of devising and implementing a constitutional principle of religious freedom has affected the actual American political community.

For almost half a century now, the Supreme Court has undertaken to supervise American public institutions to ensure conformity with the establishment clause, interpreted to contain principles such as "strict separation," "no aid to religion," "no endorsement of religion," and neutrality. Although the Court has offered a variety of rationales for its interpretation and implementation of the establishment clause, probably the most common justification has invoked the need to prevent civil strife in matters of religion.[68] In the last decade or so, this "civil peace" rationale has been refined and extended to include the "nonalienation" rationale.

During most of this period, critics have argued that the Court was battling an imaginary evil. Religion, they contended, was simply not a major source of dissension in this country.[69] Today, however, a different assessment may be indicated. Although conflict over religion still may not threaten the nation's continued existence, such conflict does seem more serious and widespread now than twenty-five or fifty years ago. In the last decade or so, the so-called religious Right has become more visible and aggressive in attempting to enter or influence politics. These efforts have provoked both resentment and resistance on the part of other groups. For example, the influence of the Christian Coalition in political campaigns in 1992 "was enough to induce virtual hysteria among watchdogs of liberal orthodoxy, such as the American Civil Liberties Union and People for the American Way."[70] The current struggle within the Republican party reflects the increase in political tension that arises from religious conflict.

Of course, there is no simple explanation for these developments. It seems fairly clear, though, that one major contributing factor has been the Supreme Court itself.[71] Noting "what appears to be a massive and unanticipated reentry of religious influence in the public domain," Harvey Cox points out that "some of this activity has definitely come in response to what its advocates define as an attack on religion by the courts and other branches of government."[72] The Court's decisions systematically eliminating all religious elements and symbols from the public schools and, somewhat less systematically, cutting off public aid to religious schools and institutions are for many religious believers evidence of an effort to impose a philosophy of secularism on public life—to exalt the "secular republic" vision of our political community while suppressing the "religious people" or "Christian nation" visions.[73] Stephen Carter has recently suggested that through both judicial decisions and academic theory that has entered legal and political culture, "[w]e are, in effect (and sometimes in so many words), telling the religiously devout that religious belief is aberrational and arbitrary and undemocratic."[74] For the religiously devout, not surprisingly, these developments and messages generate a strong sense of alienation.

As Frederick Gedicks has observed, "[t]he imposition of secularism on religious people . . . carries with it the danger of deep alienation, threatening either to marginalize religious belief or to provoke religious revolt against the imposed secular order."[75] That alienation, in turn, has contributed to the political mobilization of the religious Right, with the tensions and strife that have accompanied that mobilization. In retrospect, it seems, the Court undertook the enforcement of principles calculated to avoid remote or nonexistent evils, and in doing so it helped bring those evils into being.

It would miss the point, however, to conclude that the Court erred by choosing the wrong principles of religious freedom. To have chosen and enforced any other set of principles—principles, say, based on a "Christian nation" conception of the national community—might well have been even more divisive. The lesson from this experience, rather, is that in a pluralistic community exhibiting a considerable degree of religious and secular diversity, civil peace and inclusiveness can be achieved only imperfectly and only through compromise, cultivated tolerance, mutual forbearances, and strategic silences. In this context, the judicial imposition of *any* set of consistent and explicit principles is likely to undermine the possibilities for compromise and forbearance, and hence to aggravate the dangers of civil strife and alienation. Civil peace, in short, must be the product of prudence, not of principle imposed from above.

9

Afterword: Normative Questions

Over the past half century, judges and legal scholars have expended vast amounts of time, thought, and ink in an effort to elucidate the meaning of religious freedom. Their efforts, as I have tried to show, have not succeeded — and, indeed, given the kinds of questions they have asked and the kinds of answers they have tried to supply, could not have succeeded. This is not to say that these efforts have been wasted or that they have been unilluminating. But the judicial and academic project was calculated to produce a convincing and usable principle or theory of religious freedom, and that task has not been and could not have been accomplished.

In retrospect, this failure should not be surprising. With respect to the originalist strategy, it is common knowledge that the Constitution's framers thought that religion was a matter for the states, not for the national government, and hence that express constitutional protection for religious freedom was unnecessary. It is a familiar fact as well that discussions of the religion clauses in the First Congress and in the ratifying legislatures were sparse and apathetic. Given the well-known propensity of politicians to avoid difficult and controversial issues, why should anyone have supposed that the framers, in a relatively few minutes of congressional discussion, would have settled on any substantive principle for resolving some of the most difficult and divisive issues likely to arise in a diverse political community?

And with regard to the theoretical strategy, why was it ever realistic to suppose that the complex and fluctuating relations among the often incommensurable concerns of governments, churches, and the individual conscience could sensibly be regulated by developing and applying a uniform "principle" or "theory" of religious freedom? As Mark Howe observed, "the role of churchmen and churches in the political and moral life of the American people has always challenged theory and bewildered the defenders of constitutional rigidities."[1]

In short, judges and legal scholars have been misled because they have insisted on discovering something in the nature of a "principle" where there was no likelihood of finding one,[2] and the principles that they have purported to discover amount to "[i]llusion born of oversimplification."[3] Indeed, we may wonder why courts and scholars have persisted in this apparently hopeless quest for the constitutional principle. The answer, it seems, lies in the political and legal backdrop against which the inquiry has been conducted.

The last half century was not the first period of history in which the subject of religious freedom has been intensely discussed. Such discussions have always taken account of—and indeed have been driven by—certain recognized problems, needs, and social realities. In colonial America, the backdrop for debates about religious freedom included common but controversial practices, such as blasphemy prosecutions, religious qualifications for public office, and, most important, public subsidization of Christian clergy. Medieval discussions were driven by recurring conflicts between popes and secular rulers. In the age of Augustine the social realities that shaped thought included an empire that had formerly been pagan but had more recently officially embraced Christianity and that was threatened not only by barbarian invaders but also by religious dissenters, such as the Donatists.

In our own time, discussions of religious freedom have been powerfully influenced by a peculiarly modern factor: the institution of judicial review. Much of the influential work in this area has been performed by judges, who must necessarily relate their work to the operation and demands of judicial review. By contrast, it might seem that academicians would have the luxury of pursuing their inquiries free from the institutional pressures and constraints of judicial review. In reality, however, the overwhelming tendency of legal academicians in this country has been to write for judges—whether or not there is any reason to believe that judges are paying attention.[4] Often, to be sure, scholarly work appears to be addressed more directly to other scholars than to judges; but even then, such scholarship typically concludes with a prescription about the proper *judicial* resolution of an issue. In short, even when legal scholars are not speaking directly *to* judges, they are commonly speaking to each other *about* judges or about what judges should do. Hence, the tacit assumption underlying most legal scholarship has been that legal investigations and analyses must ultimately turn up answers or conclusions that might be useful to courts in the performance of judicial review. [5]

That assumption, in turn, helps account for the academic fixation on the notion of a "principle" of religious freedom. As noted earlier, legal scholars of various political and jurisprudential stripes have maintained that the countermajoritarian institution of judicial review is illegitimate except as it seeks to give meaning and force to constitutional principles. [6] If this assessment is true, then constitutional scholarship that merely provides insight into questions of religious freedom without distilling that insight into a judicially usable principle will have failed in its ultimate task. In this way, it seems, the background of judicial review, and of the perceived need to justify and guide the exercise of that function, has restricted the sorts of inquiries and answers that legal scholars have felt free to consider. Their virtual obsession with judicial review has led constitutional scholars to concentrate on questions that, for the reasons discussed in this book, were foreordained to produce oversimplification and confusion rather than understanding and fruitful discussion.

If this diagnosis is correct in describing the pervasively normative and court-centered character of legal discourse, then the diagnosis will predictably elicit a normative and court-centered question: What should "we" (meaning, primarily, the courts) do? If our current ways of talking about religious freedom under the Constitution are misconceived and futile, then how *should* we talk about religious freedom? More pointedly, if judicial review is appropriate only to enforce a constitutional principle, and if there is not and cannot be any constitutional principle of religious freedom, doesn't it follow that courts should simply get out of the business of protecting religious freedom altogether (except, perhaps, when the positive law on the subject is more substantive and specific than the First Amendment's religion clauses are)?

For purposes of this book, these questions pose a dilemma. It should be clear, I hope, that my objective in this book has not been to answer normative questions of this kind. On the contrary, I have suggested that the current malaise in the discourse of religious freedom is in part the product of our fixation on such questions. My purpose has been to clarify our situation by trying to explore the nature and sources of our current confusion. On the other hand, when analysis is largely critical, as mine has been, it can easily be understood as purely negative and destructive — critique merely for the sake of critique — and hence as irresponsible. Although I would disagree with this characterization — it seems to me that understanding our situation, including the futility of our present ways of talking, is a valuable achievement and an essential part of any constructive effort — it is also true that the argument of this book naturally provokes the kinds of normative questions described above. And at some point, those questions will need to be addressed.

My present response to this dilemma is, first, to insist that any prescription for a new regime of religious freedom is premature but, second, to describe, vaguely and tentatively, the lines of normative inquiry that seem naturally to proceed from the diagnosis offered in this book. That diagnosis suggests that the pressing normative question — what should "we" (or the courts) do? — is currently troublesome because of two background assumptions. The first assumption, already noted above, is that judicial review must be based on something called "principle." The second assumption is that the courts necessarily have an essential and central role to play in the realization and protection of religious freedom. Without these assumptions, the argument of this book — that there can be no constitutional principle of religious freedom — would not be especially disturbing. Abandon the first assumption, and the question "What should the courts do?" might naturally lead one to argue that the courts should protect religious freedom without purporting to be enforcing any principle. Retain the first assumption but abandon the second, and the question might generate an obvious response: In this area, courts cannot legitimately exercise the power of judicial review.

These observations suggest the possible value of rethinking the background assumptions. First, legal scholars might seriously ask whether it is so clear that judicial review must be based on principle.[7] Why has this view become so entrenched in constitutional thinking? And are there alternative accounts of judicial review?

With respect to these questions, Harold Berman's assessment of legal philosophy in this century may be illuminating. Berman describes three main classical schools of legal philosophy: legal positivism, natural law, and the historical school.[8] In this century, however, the historical school has all but disappeared:

> The historical school has been almost universally disparaged and
> has virtually disappeared from almost all jurisprudential writings

in the twentieth century, at least in England and the United States. Indeed, the almost total neglect of historical jurisprudence during the past generation — the failure even to acknowledge its existence — has crippled English and American legal philosophy. [9]

With the disappearance of historical jurisprudence, legal thinking, including thinking about judicial review, has been dominated by the positivist and natural law views.

Berman's assessment may shed light on the prevailing under-standings of the judicial role under the Constitution, including in the area of the religion clauses. Although the classification is hardly exact, originalist approaches to the religion clauses seem to be in-formed by a positivist understanding of law; the controlling question is what law, or what "principle," the enactors in fact adopted or "posited." More theoretical approaches reflect a natural law orienta-tion, with its close association of law and "reason." The burden of this book is that neither of these approaches generates a productive discourse about religious freedom: The framers did not enact into law any substantive version of religious freedom, nor does "reason" produce general or "principled" answers to questions about religious freedom. But it is at least imaginable that a full-blooded "historical" (not "originalist" in a positivist sense) approach might be more fruit-ful. Americans *have*, after all, developed and maintained beliefs about religious freedom; and even if those beliefs were not con-sciously enacted into positive law at the time of the founding, they have influenced and been embodied in our practices and traditions. Perhaps a historical approach could distill these different, develop-ing beliefs and traditions into a usable law of religious freedom — or even, conceivably, into some modest but usable principles — that would be "constitutional" not in the standard positivist sense or in the theoretical or natural law sense, but rather in the sense of being "constitutive" of our political community.

This possibility seems worth exploring. For now, I will merely note two caveats. First, the effort to squeeze constitutional law out of "history and tradition" confronts familiar difficulties. [10] In the realm of religious freedom, for instance, it seems unlikely that his-torical research can discover any single or unified tradition; our history has been and continues to be marked, rather, by earnest, occasionally violent disagreements over the proper relationship be-tween government and religion. Those conflicts manifest them-selves, among other places, in the cases and controversies that courts are asked to decide, and it is unclear how courts can resolve such conflicts by appealing to tradition when the tradition itself reflects the same divisions that the cases present.

It is possible that this problem might be partially overcome by a relatively modest and specific use of tradition. If tradition is used to support ambitious principles such as "no public aid to religion" or "no governmental endorsement of religion," for example, then tradition will almost inevitably yield conflicting results. Our history will reveal disagreements about whether the supposed "principle" is accepted or, if it is, about what the principle means; and judicial invocation of one aspect of the tradition will merely be favoring one constituency over others. But it is possible that more modest and narrow principles could be plausibly derived from tradition. Our history speaks with conflicting voices on the question whether government should "aid" religion, but it may convincingly support the idea that government should not recognize any particular denomination as the official state church, or that government should not require, or forbid, participation in particular religion movements. Precisely because they are narrower and less controversial, of course, these more humble maxims are less likely to be violated; consequently, they would not provide frequent grounds for judicial review.

A second caveat is that even if historical jurisprudence might provide a helpful *descriptive account* of constitutional law, [11] it is less clear that this kind of jurisprudence could provide *legitimation* for the practice of judicial review. The historical account seems best exemplified by the common law tradition, but in that tradition courts normally did not consider themselves authorized to overrule laws enacted by the legislature. [12] Similarly, in a provocative article written almost two decades ago, Henry Monaghan proposed that many of the Supreme Court's decisions could best be understood as a form of "constitutional common law." [13] But Monaghan explained that by this view the courts' decisions could not be regarded as superior to congressional enactments; rather, constitutional common law would be "subject to amendment, modification, or even reversal by Congress." [14] It may not be an accident, in other words, that accounts of judicial review have tended to arise from either positivist or naturalist premises; a historical account, while illuminating, might have difficulty in explaining why courts should have the power to negate statutes by which an elected legislature attempts to embody or to alter tradition. [15]

In short, the prevailing assumption that judicial review is illegitimate except insofar as it is pursuant to "principle" warrants closer examination, but that examination might end up by reaffirming the assumption. Whether or not one reaches that conclusion, the second background assumption — that courts must necessarily play an active part in the achievement and preservation of religious freedom — also deserves scrutiny. We should take seriously, in other words, the possibility that judicial intervention under the Constitution into matters of religious freedom *is* illegitimate or unjustified. Is it clear that such a conclusion would be so tragic?

Some other countries — England, for example — have foregone the institution of judicial review, and indeed have formally maintained an established church, without any major discernible diminution of religious freedom.[16] Moreover, we ought to remember that in this country every state had rid itself of its official religious establishment within a few decades of the founding — without judicial compulsion. Indeed, Judge Arlin Adams and Charles Emmerich point out that "[f]rom the republic's inception to the early decades of the twentieth century, religious liberty emerged largely without the participation of the federal judiciary."[17] During that period, John Noonan observes, the religion clauses had "absolutely no impact" on the states and "no apparent impact on Congress and the president."[18]

Since entering the field, moreover, the Court has done little to shield religious freedom against what might seem to be the most powerful governmental threat to it — that is, the national government. John Noonan points out:

> The United States Supreme Court never found a law made by Congress to infringe religious liberty. The blandness of academic acolytes of the Court conceals this dismaying fact. The Court has been portrayed as the champion of religious liberty. It has not been the champion against the co-equal branch of government, whose power the [First] Amendment had been written to curb.[19]

On the state level, of course, the courts have invalidated many laws and practices that they thought to be incompatible with religious freedom. Probably everyone (including me) can point to some of these judicial decisions that seem salutary — and to other decisions that seem unfortunate or wrongheaded. Granted that some of the decisions have been good ones (and there is no consensus, of course, on which decisions those are), is it clear that there has been a significant net gain?

The question is complicated by the fact that a few decisions have invalidated, on grounds of constitutional principle, programs that by consensus were performing valuable social functions. The Court's decisions striking down educational programs of proven effectiveness in helping disadvantaged children are perhaps the leading example.[20] Any cost-benefit assessment of the overall corpus of religion clause jurisprudence would have to take into account the acknowledged costs of these decisions.

The curtailment of judicial review under the religion clauses would not mean, of course, that religious freedom would disappear from the public agenda. The imposing presence of a judicial overseer may have lulled us into forgetting that religious freedom is properly the concern of citizens and governmental institutions generally.[21] To be sure, leaving religious freedom to the political process has its risks. Most obviously, unpopular religious minorities may have little power in the political process.[22] On the other hand, it is arguable that the political process is more responsive to religious freedom concerns than the courts have been. With regard to the issue of state regulation of religious schools, for instance, Neal Devins has recently argued that "[j]udicial attempts to resolve this dispute have been truly unsatisfactory."[23] But "[t]he state political process . . . is as a matter of political necessity extraordinarily sensitive to religious liberty concerns."[24]

Experience with free exercise accommodation may support this point. Although before *Employment Division v. Smith* (the peyote decision) the federal judiciary theoretically stood ready to require free exercise accommodations in some cases, in reality such accommodation almost always came not from the courts[25] but rather from legislatures. The most significant accommodations to religious freedom are found in state and federal tax exemptions, in the military conscription law, and in federal employment statutes—all legislatively adopted. Indeed, courts seemed more inclined to invalidate legislatively mandated accommodation on establishment grounds than to order such accommodation on free exercise grounds.[26] This experience suggests that a judicial withdrawal from the field might not detract from, and indeed might amount to a net gain for, religious freedom.[27]

More generally, Gerard Bradley has argued that the principal protection for religious freedom has always been in a pluralistic political process rather than in constitutional doctrine.[28] Bradley's invocation of pluralism recalls the conclusion reached by Mark DeWolfe Howe a generation earlier. Criticizing "the Court's current inclination to extract a few homespun absolutes from the complexities of a pluralistic tradition," Howe suggested that "in these matters the living practices of the American people bespeak our basic constitutional commitments more accurately than do the dogmatic pronouncements of the justices."[29] And Howe wondered whether the justices "may waste the nation's inheritance if they constantly dip into principle."[30]

These conjectures are meant to be just that—conjectures. I present them only to suggest that the background assumptions that may make the argument of this book seem threatening should not be taken for granted or left (as they sometimes are) in the category of propositions that are beyond serious challenge. But I want to conclude by reiterating that my purpose in this book has not been to advocate any particular version of religious freedom, much less to prescribe the optimal method for realizing religious freedom or to pronounce on the role, if any, that courts should play in this area. On the contrary, I have tried to show that investigations of religious freedom in the legal academy have been crippled precisely by an excessive eagerness to prescribe to courts.[31] Discussions of religious freedom will likely be more fruitful when scholars relax their obsession with judicial review and relinquish their accompanying demand that the meaning of religious freedom be cabined within the narrow confines of a constitutional "principle."

NOTES

Chapter 1

1. *See* Donald L. Drakeman, Church-State Constitutional Issues 83 (1991) (noticing "the many calls for new and better approaches").

2. Employment Division v. Smith, 494 U.S. 872 (1990). Nadine Strossen observes that the decision "was enormously upsetting . . . to a wide spectrum of religious leaders and constitutional scholars around the country." Nadine Strossen, "Justice Brennan and the Religion Clauses," 11 Pace L. Rev. 491, 499 (1991).

3. Under the *Lemon* test, a law challenged under the establishment clause needed to satisfy three requirements. "First, the statute must have a secular legislative purpose; second, its principal or primary effect must be one that neither advances nor inhibits religion . . . ; finally, the statute must not foster 'an excessive government entanglement with religion.'" Lemon v. Kurtzman, 403 U.S. 602, 612–13 (1971). In Lee v. Weisman, 112 S. Ct. 2649 (1992), only four justices actually endorsed the *Lemon* test. Hence, some scholars conclude the *Lemon* test has already effectively been abandoned. *See, e.g.*, Michael Stokes Paulsen, "*Lemon* Is Dead," 43 Case W. Res. L. Rev. 795 (1993). *But see* Daniel O. Conkle, "*Lemon* Lives," 43 Case W. Res. L. Rev. 865 (1993).

4. Douglas Laycock, "A Survey of Religious Liberty in the United States," 47 Ohio St. L.J. 409, 450 (1986).

5. John Mansfield, "The Religion Clauses of the First Amendment and the Philosophy of the Constitution," 72 Cal. L. Rev. 846, 848 (1984).

6. Lynch v. Donnelly, 465 U.S. 668 (1984). For a list of some of the more forceful and colorful criticisms, see Steven D. Smith, "Symbols, Perceptions, and Doctrinal Illusions: Establishment Neutrality and the 'No Endorsement' Test," 86 Mich. L. Rev. 266, 269–70 (1987).

7. This phenomenon is discussed at greater length in chapter 8.

8. Aguilar v. Felton, 473 U.S. 402, 415 (1985) (Powell, J., concurring, and quoting with approval the court of appeals decision). Arguments urging the fanciful nature of the grounds of invalidation are energetically presented in Justice Sandra Day O'Connor's dissenting opinion. *Id.* at 421–

31. O'Connor concluded that for thousands of disadvantaged children, "the Court's decision is tragic. The Court deprives them of a program that offers a meaningful chance of success in life, and it does so on the untenable theory that public school teachers (most of whom are of different faiths than their students) are likely to start teaching religion merely because they have walked across the threshold of a parochial school." *Id.* at 431.

9. Mary Ann Glendon & Raul F. Yanes, "Structural Free Exercise," 90 Mich. L. Rev. 477, 481 (1991).

10. *Id.* at 491–92.

11. *Id.* at 547.

12. 330 U.S. 1 (1947).

13. For major criticisms of the Court's constructions of history, see Gerard V. Bradley, Church-State Relationships in America (1987); Robert L. Cord, Separation of Church and State: Historical Fact and Current Fiction (1982); Mark Dewolfe Howe, The Garden and the Wilderness (1965).

14. Michael Stokes Paulsen, "Religion, Equality, and the Constitution: An Equal Protection Approach to Establishment Clause Adjudication," 61 Notre Dame L. Rev. 311, 314 (1986).

15. *See, e.g.*, Editorial, "Churches and Politics: The IRS Cracks Down," 46 Church & State 13 (109) (May 1993) (asserting that Pat Robertson, Billy Falling, and others "seek a theocracy" and must be resisted by "Americans who believe in real religious freedom"); Joseph L. Conn, "Unholy Matrimony," 46 Church & State 4 (76) (Apr. 1993) (arguing that conservative Catholics and evangelicals "share a profound hostility to the principle of church-state separation"). *See also* Gregg Ivers, Redefining the First Freedom: The Supreme Court and the Consolidation of State Power 8 (1993) (asserting that "conservative organizations" are engaged in an "assault on church-state separation").

16. *See, e.g.*, Leo Pfeffer, Church, State, and Freedom 82 (1953).

17. *Id.*

18. Douglas Laycock, "Original Intent and the Constitution Today," *in* The First Freedom: Religion and the Bill of Rights 87, 89 (James E. Wood, Jr., ed. 1990). *See also* Paulsen, *supra* note 3, at 840 (explaining that graduation prayer is unconstitutional, despite its support in history and tradition, because "it may not have occurred to the founding generation that familiar practices violated constitutional principles for the simple reason that the practices were so familiar").

19. *See, e.g.*, County of Allegheny v. ACLU, 109 S. Ct. 3086, 3099 (1989) (plurality opinion); Wallace v. Jaffree, 472 U.S. 38, 52–53 (1985).

20. Massachusetts Constitution of 1780, art. 2, *reprinted in* The American Constitutions and Religion 40 (Conrad Henry Moehlman comp., 1938).

21. *See* Winthrop Hudson, "Liberty, Both Civil and Religious," *in* The Lively Experiment Continued 71, 81–84 (Jerald C. Brauer ed., 1987).

22. Mass. Const. of 1780, art. 3, *supra* note 20, at 40–41.

23. *Quoted in* Timothy L. Hall, "Religion, Equality, and Difference," 65 Temp. L. Rev. 1, 24 (1992).

24. 3 Thomas Aquinas, Summa Theologica 2.2.10.8, at 1213 (Fathers of the Dominican Province trans., 1981).

25. John Locke, "A Letter Concerning Toleration," *in* John Locke on Politics and Education 17, 57–58 (Classics Club ed. 1947).

26. Robert L. Cord, "Founding Intentions and the Establishment Clause: Harmonizing Accommodation and Separation," 10 Harv. J.L. & Pub. Pol'y 47, 49 (1987).

27. *See id.* at 50; Thomas J. Curry, The First Freedoms: Church and State in America to the Passage of the First Amendment 217 (1986).

28. Everson v. Board of Education, 330 U.S. 1, 18 (1947).

29. *See, e.g.*, Mueller v. Allen, 463 U.S. 388 (1983) (approving indirect aid to parochial schools); Wolman v. Walter, 433 U.S. 229 (1977) ("parochiaid"); Marsh v. Chambers, 463 U.S. 783 (1983) (upholding legislative prayer); Lynch v. Donnelly, 465 U.S. 668 (1984) (nativity scene); Bowen v. Kendrick, 487 U.S. 589 (1988) (counseling).

30. *See, e.g.*, Curry, *supra* note 27, at 219. T. Jeremy Gunn, A Standard for Repair: The Establishment Clause, Equality, and Natural Rights 184–96 (1992); John Swomley, Religious Liberty and the Secular State 127 (1987).

31. Douglas Laycock, "'Nonpreferential' Aid to Religion: A False Claim About Original Intent," 27 Wm. & Mary L. Rev. 875, 919 (1986).

32. Everson v. Board of Education, 330 U.S. 1, 19 (1947) (Jackson, J., dissenting).

33. Philip B. Kurland, "The Religion Clauses and the Burger Court," 34 Cath. U. L. Rev. 1, 11–13 (1984).

34. Douglas Laycock, "Equal Access and Moments of Silence: The Equal Status of Religious Speech by Private Speakers," 81 Nw. U. L. Rev. 1, 8 (1986).

35. *See* "Supreme Court Hears Oral Arguments in Key Church-State Case," 46 Church & State 14 (86) (Apr. 1993) (describing Rehnquist and Scalia as the Court's "antiseparationist wing").

36. Isaiah Berlin, The Crooked Timber of Humanity 37 (Henry Hardy ed., 1992).

37. John T. Noonan, Jr., The Believer and the Powers That Are 41–42 (1987).

38. *Id.* at 37.

39. *See* Pfeffer, *supra* note 16, at 13–20.

40. *See* Laycock, *supra* note 31, at 913–19; Paulsen, *supra* note 3, at 840.

41. *Cf.* Gerard V. Bradley, "Protecting Religious Liberty: Judicial and Legislative Responsibilities," 42 DePaul L. Rev. 253, 256 (1992) ("There is not only a plurality of religions but, not accidentally, a plurality of conceptions of religious liberty.").

42. *See supra*, notes 18–19, 30–31 and accompanying text.

43. For a critical discussion of this judicial style and mode of thought, see Robert F. Nagel, "The Formulaic Constitution," 84 Mich. L. Rev. 165 (1985).

44. 330 U.S. 1 (1947).

45. Perhaps the leading figure in this effort (although hardly the only one) has been Leo Pfeffer. *See, e.g.*, Leo Pfeffer, God, Caesar, and the Constitution (1975); Pfeffer, *supra* note 16.

46. *See* studies cited *supra* note 13.

47. The first careful attempt to ascertain the original meaning of the free exercise clause was Michael W. McConnell, "The Origins and Historical Understanding of the Free Exercise of Religion," 103 Harv. L. Rev. 1409 (1990). Studies critical of McConnell's interpretation include Philip A. Hamburger, "A Constitutional Right of Religious Exemption: An Historical Perspective," 60 Geo. Wash. L. Rev. 915 (1992); Gerard V. Bradley, "Beguiled: Free Exercise Exemptions and the Siren Song of Liberalism," 20 Hofstra L. Rev. 245 (1991).

48. *See, e.g.*, Paul Kauper, Religion and the Constitution 47 (1964) ("The search for original meaning and historical purpose underlying this language has yielded inconclusive results, and it would not be profitable to explore this matter in detail.").

49. Lee v. Weisman, 112 S. Ct. 2649, 2667, 2668–71, 2672–73 (1992) (Souter, J., concurring).

50. *See, e.g.*, Bradley, *supra* note 47, at 250 ("Originalists properly seek in the historical materials an intelligible principle capable of guiding contemporary decision."). In this respect, religion clause originalists adopt the course favored by leading constitutional originalists in general. *See, e.g.*, Robert H. Bork, The Tempting of America 143–60 (1990); Michael J. Perry, The Constitution in the Courts: Law or Politics, ch. 3 (1994).

51. Donald Drakeman points out that "[n]early everyone who has tried to interpret the establishment clause, including the Supreme Court, is an originalist of one sort or another and has assumed the authority of the founders' intent." Drakeman, *supra* note 1, at 98.

52. Even so, perhaps for the reasons discussed in the text, legal discourse exhibits a simplifying or reductionist impulse. Many discussions seem to assume that the eligible candidates are limited to a handful of, or even to two, principal positions, commonly referred, to as the "separationist" and "accommodationist" positions. *See* Robert L. Cord & Howard Ball, "The Separation of Church and State: A Debate," 1987 Utah L. Rev. 895, 920 (describing the "[t]wo views on the relationship between church and state [that] have emerged" as the "narrow accommodationist view" and the "broader, strict separationist view"). *See also* Richard H. Jones, "Accommodationist and Separationist Ideals in Supreme Court Establishment Clause Decisions," 28 J. Church & State 193 (1986); Richard Morgan, The Politics of Religious Conflict: Church and State in America 49–68 (2d ed. 1980).

Chapter 2

1. Eric Foner expresses a common view when he observes that "[i]n an age of semiotics and deconstruction, . . . there is something naive, almost quaint, in the idea that any text, including the Constitution, possesses a single, easily ascertainable meaning." Eric Foner, "The Supreme Court's Legal History," 23 Rutgers L.J. 243, 243 (1992). For an application of the standard objections to originalism to the religion clauses, see mark v. Tushnet, "The Constitution of Religion," 18 Conn. L. Rev. 701, 706–08 (1986).

2. For a list of scholars who have acknowledged this element, see Note, "Rethinking the Incorporation of the Establishment Clause," 105 Harv. L. Rev. 1700, 1703 n. 25 (1992) [hereinafter Harvard Note].

3. The issue and effect of "incorporation" are considered more directly in chapter 4.

4. Joseph M. Snee, "Religious Disestablishment and the Fourteenth Amendment," 1954 Wash. U. L.Q. 371, 389 (emphasis added). Snee believed that the substantive right was embodied in the free exercise clause and that the purpose of the establishment clause was wholly federalist. *Id.* More recently, Akhil Amar and a student note in the *Harvard Law Review* have taken a similar position. *See* Akhil Reed Amar, "The Bill of Rights as a Constitution," 100 Yale L.J. 1131, 1158–59 (1991); Harvard Note, *supra* note 2, at 1717–18. By contrast, most scholars, as well as the Supreme Court itself, have assumed that the establishment clause also contained both a federalist element and a substantive right or principle. Either way, judges and scholars have believed themselves free — and even obliged — to elaborate the scope and meaning of the substantive right or principle supposedly contained in the religion clauses.

5. Mark Dewolfe Howe, The Garden and the Wilderness 29 (1965).

6. *See, e.g.*, Tom Gerety, "Legal Gardening: Mark Dewolfe Howe on Church and State: A Retrospective Essay," 38 Stan. L. Rev. 595, 596 (1986) (asserting that Howe's book "remains by far the best piece of scholarship in the field of church and state").

> 7. For more than fourteen hundred years . . . it was a universal assumption that the stability of the social order and the safety of the state demanded the religious solidarity of all the people in one church. Every responsible thinker, every ecclesiastic, every ruler and statesman who gave the matter any attention, held to this as an axiom. There was no political or social philosophy which did not build upon this assumption. . . . [A]ll, with no exceptions other than certain disreputable and "subversive" heretics, believed firmly that religious solidarity in the one recognized church was essential to social and political stability.

Sidney E. Mead, The Lively Experiment: The Shaping of Christianity in America 60 (1963) (quoting Winfred E. Garrison, "Characteristics of

American Organized Religion," 256 Annals Am. Acad. Pol. & Soc. Sci. 14, 16–17 (1948)).

8. *See* Patricia U. Bonomi, Under the Cope of Heaven: Religion, Society, and Politics in Colonial America 14 (1986) ("Only through . . . [an established church], so the [colonial] leaders believed, might the colonists ward off the evils of religious strife. . . . "); Edwin S. Gaustad, "Colonial Religion and Liberty of Conscience," *in* The Virginia Statute for Religious Freedom: Its Evolution and Consequences in American History 23 (Merrill D. Peterson & Robert C. Vaughn eds., 1988) [hereinafter Virginia Statute] ("The majority . . . knew that society prospered, the state advanced, and the gospel was made secure only as sacred and secular realms coalesced.").

9. Mass. Const. of 1780, *reprinted in* The American Constitutions and Religion 40–41 (Conrad Henry Moehlman comp., 1938).

10. Timothy Dwight, "Letter V: Vindication of the Establishment of the Public Worship of God by Law," *in* 4 Travels in New England and New York 283, 284–85 (Barbara Solomon ed., 1969) (New Haven 1822).

11. *See* Steven D. Smith, "The Rise and Fall of Religious Freedom in Constitutional Discourse," 140 U. Pa. L. Rev. 149, 154–62 (1991). Thomas Curry's presentation of the major opposing positions in the Virginia debate over religious assessments approximates this description of the "traditional" and "voluntarist" positions:

> Proponents of a general assessment . . . believed that religion was absolutely necessary to sustain the moral fiber of society, and that the state should promote it as a means to that end. Evangelical opponents of a general assessment agreed on the indispensability of religion. . . . For them, [however,] the cause of true religion could be furthered only by the grace of God, and State attempts to advance it would result in the creation of a bureaucratic state religion.

Thomas J. Curry, The First Freedoms: Church and State in America to the Passage of the First Amendment 138 (1986).

12. *See, e.g.,* Thomas Jefferson, "Notes on Virginia," *in* The Life and Selected Writings of Thomas Jefferson 278 (Adrienne Koch & William Peden eds., 1944) ("And can the liberties of a nation be thought secure when we have removed their only firm basis, a conviction in the minds of the people that these liberties are the gift of God?").

13. Robert Baird, Religion in the United States of America 230 (Arno Press 1969) (1844).

14. *Id.* at 241. Although not ascribing this antireligious animosity to Jefferson, William Miller concludes that Jefferson "held as a central tenet that religion and morality could be separated: that virtue did not require the underpinning of religion, and indeed that it was weak and misleading to

think that it did." William Lee Miller, "The Moral Project of the American Founders," *in* Articles of Faith, Articles of Peace: The Religious Liberty Clauses and the American Public Philosophy 17, 34 (James Davison Hunter & Os Guinness eds., 1990) [hereinafter Articles of Faith]. For a contrary view, see Thomas E. Buckley, "The Political Theology of Thomas Jefferson," *in* Virginia Statute, *supra* note 8, at 75, 77 (arguing that "Jefferson enunciated a civic faith clearly related to and dependent on a transcendent God"). It is possible, of course, that Jefferson's thinking on these matters was not entirely stable or consistent. *See* Daniel L. Dreisbach, "Thomas Jefferson and Bills Number 82–86 of the Revision of the Law of Virginia: New Light on the Jeffersonian Model of Church-State Relations," 69 N.C. L. Rev. 159, 210 (1990).

15. Curry asserts that Jefferson and a few contemporaries doubted the necessity of religion for a healthy society, but "few Virginians would have agreed with them." Curry, *supra* note 11, at 142.

16. "It seems undeniable that the First Amendment operated, and was intended to operate, to protect from Congressional interference the varying state policies of church establishments." Wilbur Katz, Religion and American Constitutions 9 (1964). *See also* Paul Kauper, Religion and the Constitution 46 (1964).

17. Daniel O. Conkle, "Toward a General Theory of the Establishment Clause," 82 Nw. U. L. Rev. 1113, 1133 (1988).

18. *See, e.g.*, Harvard Note, *supra* note 2; Snee, *supra* note 4.

19. *See* Barron v. Baltimore, 32 U.S. (7 Pet.) 243 (1833) (holding Bill of Rights inapplicable to the states).

20. Thus, Gerard Bradley may be correct that terms used in the religion clauses had acquired meanings at the state level and that the framers and ratifiers of the First Amendment intended to use these terms in the understood or conventional sense. Gerard V. Bradley, "Beguiled: Free Exercise Exemptions and the Siren Song of Liberalism," 20 Hofstra L. Rev. 245, 305 (1991). In short, the religion clauses may have denied to the national government some of the same substantive powers that some state constitutions denied to state governments. Even if this observation is true, however, it does not follow that these powers were denied *for the same purpose* at the national and state levels. Virginia law might have denied the state the power to establish a religion because established religion violated that state's understanding of religious freedom, whereas the federal Constitution may have denied the same power to the national government for an entirely different reason — that is, because the choice whether to maintain an established church was a matter for the states, not the national government, to decide.

21. *See, e.g.*, Leonard W. Levy, The Establishment Clause: Religion and the First Amendment 79 (1986):

> The debate [on the proposed religion clauses] was sometimes irrelevant, usually apathetic and unclear. Ambiguity, brev-

ity, and imprecision in thought and expression characterize the comments of the few members who spoke. That the House understood the debate, cared deeply about its outcome, or shared a common understanding of the finished amendment seems doubtful.

Not even Madison himself, dutifully carrying out his pledge to secure amendments, seems to have troubled to do more than was necessary to get something adopted in order to satisfy the popular clamor for a bill of rights. . . .

22. Gerard V. Bradley, Church-State Relationships in America 114–17 (1987) [hereinafter Bradley, Relationships].

23. Rhys Isaac, "'The Rage of Malice of the Old Serpent Devil': The Dissenters and the Making and Remaking of the Virginia Statute for Religious Freedom," *in* Virginia Statute, *supra* note 8, at 139, 146.

24. These arguments must to some extent be extrapolated from what scholars have said on related questions because the precise premise under consideration here—that is, the assumption that the religion clauses had *some* substantive content independent of their federalism—has largely been taken for granted rather than argued for directly.

25. *See* Gerard V. Bradley, "The No Religious Test Clause and the Constitution of Religious Liberty: A Machine That Has Gone of Itself, 37 Case W. Res. L. Rev. 674, 713 (1987) [hereinafter Bradley, Test Clause] ("The federal government undoubtedly had power 'over religion' in the territories, the military, Indian relations, and the District of Columbia.").

26. Answering this question was not immediately imperative because, as John Nowak points out, before 1868 the Supreme Court did not rely on the Bill of Rights to limit the authority of *either* the states *or* the national government—the *Dred Scott* case being the one notable exception. John E. Nowak, "The 'Sixty Something' Anniversary of the Bill of Rights," 1992 U. Ill. L. Rev. 445, 450. When the issue was presented decades later in Reynolds v. United States, 98 U.S. 145 (1878), the Supreme Court assumed that the free exercise clause restricted the United States government in its administration of the territories. As an analytical matter, however, that assumption was superfluous to the decision because the Court held that the federal antipolygamy law did not violate the free exercise clause in any event.

27. *See* Michael W. McConnell, "The Origins and Historical Understanding of the Free Exercise of Religion," 103 Harv. L. Rev. 1409, 1477 (1990) ("There were two strands to the Federalist argument against a free exercise amendment. First, under the Constitution, the new federal government was not given any powers to pass laws affecting religion."). *See also* Levy, *supra* note 21, at 74 ("As at the Constitutional Convention a widespread understanding existed in the states during the ratification con-

troversy that the new central government would have no power whatever to legislate on the subject of religion.").

28. *Quoted in* McConnell, *supra* note 27, at 1477. In a similar vein, Richard Dobbs Spaight of North Carolina insisted: "As to the subject of religion . . . [n]o power is given to the general government to interfere with it at all. Any act of Congress on this subject would be a usurpation." *Quoted in* Levy, *supra* note 21, at 66.

29. The recorded House debate on what became the religion clauses is reported at 1 Annals of Cong. 729–31. Discussion in the Senate was not recorded. The House debate was brief enough that secondary sources can conveniently quote it in full. *See* Curry, *supra* note 11, at 200–02; Levy, *supra* note 21, at 77–79; 5 The Founders' Constitution 92–93 (Philip B. Kurland & Ralph Lerner eds., 1987). I will reference the report by Curry, whose explanatory discussion is also helpful and, in my view, less tendentious than some other treatments.

30. *See* Curry, *supra* note 11, at 200.

30. *See id.* at 200–01.

32. Daniel A. Farber & Suzanna Sherry, A History of the American Constitution 231 (1990) (quoting Madison).

33. *See generally id.* at 226, 231–32.

34. T. Jeremy Gunn, A Standard for Repair: The Establishment Clause, Equality, and Natural Rights 166–67 (1992).

35. Farber & Sherry, *supra* note 32, at 232 (quoting Vining).

36. *See* Robert L. Cord, Separation of Church and State: Historical Fact and Current Fiction 38–39, 47, 57–80, 261–70 (1982).

37. *See id.*

38. *See id.* at 262, 267–68. *See also* Douglas Laycock, "'Nonpreferential' Aid to Religion: A False Claim About Original Intent," 27 Wm. & Mary L. Rev. 875, 915 (1986).

39. *See* Bradley, Test Clause, *supra* note 25, at 713.

40. *See* Paul Finkleman, "The Ten Amendments as a Declaration of Rights," 16 S. Ill. U. L.J. 351, 382–85 (1992) (discussing how Madison's encounter with Baptist minister John Leland convinced him of the sincerity of the concern that the Constitution might threaten religious freedom).

41. Laycock, *supra* note 38, at 909. *See also* Bradley, Test Clause, *supra* note 25, at 713 ("What matters is this: the first amendment is simply inexplicable except against a background in which the federal government is believed to have power over religious practices in the states.").

42. *See* John F. Wilson, "Religion, Political Culture, and the Law," 41 DePaul L. Rev. 821, 824 (1992) (arguing that "the burden of the two religion clauses . . . was to make explicit what was already assumed, namely that religion was a subject beyond the power of Congress to regulate."). *See also* Gunn, *supra* note 34, at 66 ("None suggested that the First Amendment denied to Congress a power that it otherwise had. The amend-

ment only articulated, underscored, and publicized the fact that the government had no power to establish religion.").

43. *See* Akhil Reed Amar, "Anti-Federalists, *The Federalist Papers*, and the Big Argument for Union," 16 Harv. J.L. & Pub. Pol'y 111, 115 (1993) (footnotes omitted):

> The First Amendment intentionally inverted the language of the Necessary and Proper Clause, which stated that *"Congress shall have Power To . . . make all Laws* which shall be necessary and proper. . . . " Note how the First Amendment, which read unlike any other, tracked and reversed this language: *"Congress shall make no law . . . ,"* meaning that Congress simply had no enumerated power over either speech or religion.

44. *See* Curry, *supra* note 11, at 201 (emphasis added).

45. Bradley, Relationships, *supra* note 22, at 96 ("If Levy is correct [that the Constitution denied Congress all power over religion], why then did the First Congress ultimately *reject* Livermore's proposed 'no laws touching religion'?").

46. Proponents and critics of this position have argued at length about the significance of earlier drafts that were not finally adopted. Some of these drafts appear to express a "nonpreferentialist" view, and proponents of this position accordingly maintain that the drafts express the intended meaning of the establishment clause. *See, e.g.*, Cord, *supra* note 36, at 5–10. Conversely, critics argue that since these drafts were not ultimately adopted, the natural conclusion is that Congress *rejected* the "nonpreferentialist" view. *See* Laycock, *supra* note 38, at 879–83. Still other scholars reject both inferences, believing the changes in language to have been mainly stylistic in nature. *See* Curry, *supra* note 11, at 207–15. For a recent analysis of these drafts that attempts to refine and defend the "no preference" construction, see Rodney K. Smith, "Nonpreferentialism in Establishment Clause Analysis: A Response to Professor Laycock," 65 St. John's L. Rev. 245, 251–63 (1991).

47. *See* Curry, *supra* note 11, at 201–02.

48. *See* Gunn, *supra* note 34, at 59–65. Indeed, Bradley himself hints that the revision in language may not have reflected any substantive disagreement with the Livermore proposal: "[T]he temper of the entire House may be gauged by the conjunction of the Livermore and Ames version on August 20. In passing Ames's proposal instead of Livermore's without extended debate, the motivation of Livermore's proposal to leave state regimes undisturbed no doubt underlay the Ames language." Bradley, Relationships, *supra* note 22, at 92.

49. In addition, what became the free exercise clause adopted the language of "free exercise [of religion]" rather than "rights of conscience." For a discussion of the possible significance of this change, see McConnell, *supra* note 27, at 1488–1500.

50. *See* Cord, *supra* note 36, at 23.

51. Madison wrote to Jefferson that in the proposed Bill of Rights "everything of a controvertible nature" had been "studiously avoided." His congressional colleagues' understanding of this fact is reflected in their assessments of the amendments as "a few milk and water amendments" (Pierce Butler, George Mason), a "tub or a number of tubs to the whale" (George Clymer), "nonsense" (Robert Morris), "trash" (Fisher Ames), "anodyne to the discontented" (Edmund Randolph), and "little better than whip-syllabub, frothy and full of wind, formed only to please the palate" (Aedanus Burke). *Quoted in* Bradley, Relationships, *supra* note 22, at 88.

Chapter 3

1. *See, e.g.*, Note, "Rethinking the Incorporation of the Establishment Clause," 105 Harv. L. Rev. 1700, 1717–18 (1992); Joseph M. Snee, "Religious Disestablishment and the Fourteenth Amendment," 1954 Wash. U. L.Q. 371, 373, 389.

2. Akhil Reed Amar, "The Bill of Rights as a Constitution," 100 Yale L.J. 1131, 1159 (1991).

3. Kenneth Karst explains:

From the 1960s through the 1980s, commentators regularly remarked on the "tension" between the two religion clauses of the First Amendment. The Free Exercise Clause, vigorously enforced, seemed to command religion-based exemptions from at least some regulatory laws of general application. Yet, the Establishment clause, vigorously enforced, seemed to forbid such exemptions. Some state and local officials saw the religion clauses of the First Amendment as the jaws of a vise, tightening around the area of legislative discretion.

Kenneth L. Karst, "The First Amendment, the Politics of Religion, and the Symbols of Government," 27 Harv. C.R.-C.L. L. Rev. 503, 505 (1992) (footnote omitted).

4. *See, e.g.*, Douglas Laycock, "Towards a General Theory of the Religion Clauses: The Case of Church Labor Relations and the Right to Church Autonomy," 81 Colum. L. Rev. 1373, 1378–88 (1981); Ira C. Lupu, "Keeping the Faith: Religion, Equality, and Speech in the U.S. Constitution," 18 Conn. L. Rev. 739 (1986).

5. John T. Noonan, Jr., "Quota of Imps," *in* The Virginia Statute for Religious Freedom: Its Evolution and Consequences in American History 171, 192 (Merrill D. Peterson & Robert C. Vaughn eds., 1988).

6. *See* Philip B. Kurland, "The Irrelevance of the Constitution: The Religion Clauses of the First Amendment and the Supreme Court," 24 Vill. L. Rev. 3, 9 (1984); Leo Pfeffer, "Freedom and/or Separation: The Constitional Dilemma of the First Amendment," 64 Minn. L. Rev. 561,

564–66 (1980). Donald Gianella asserted that the framers did not perceive any tension between the clauses, although he regarded this as an oversight on their part. Donald Gianella, "Religious Liberty, Nonestablishment, and Doctrinal Development, Part I. The Religious Liberty Guarantee," 80 Harv. L. Rev. 1381, 1389 (1967).

7. T. Jeremy Gunn, A Standard for Repair: The Establishment Clause, Equality, and Natural Rights 50 (1992).

8. Thomas J. Curry, The First Freedoms: Church and State in America to the Passage of the First Amendment 216–17 (1986).

9. Mary Ann Glendon & Raul F. Yanes, "Structural Free Exercise," 90 Mich. L. Rev. 477, 478, 540 (1991).

10. *See* Thomas McCoy & Gary Kurtz, "A Unifying Theory for the Religion Clauses of the First Amendment," 39 Vand. L. Rev. 249, 253 (1986) (arguing that religion clauses should be treated as a single conceptual unit); Richard John Neuhaus, "A New Order of Religious Freedom," 60 Geo. Wash. L. Rev. 620, 627 (1992) ("There are not two religion clauses. There is but one Religion Clause."); John T. Noonan, Jr., "The End of Free Exercise?," 42 DePaul L. Rev. 567, 567 (1992); Michael A. Paulsen, "Religion, Equality, and the Constitution: An Equal Protection Approach to Establishment Clause Adjudication," 61 Notre Dame L. Rev. 311, 313, 351 (1986) (similar argument). *Cf.* The Williamsburg Charter, *reprinted in* 8 J.L. & Rel. 5, 15 (1990) ("[T]he two clauses are essentially one provision for preserving religious liberty."); Pfeffer, *supra* note 6, at 564 (asserting that "the religion clauses of the first amendment encompass a unitary guaranty of separation and freedom").

11. I do not mean to imply that these commentators endorse the jurisdictional construction defended here. While agreeing that the clauses represent a unitary provision, these scholars assume that this provision contains a substantive right or principle of religious freedom.

12. For an overview, see Gerard V. Bradley, "The No Religious Test Clause and the Constitution of Religious Liberty: A Machine That Has Gone of Itself," 37 Case W. Res. L. Rev. 674, 681–83 (1987).

13. *See* Morton Borden, Jews, Turks, and Infidels 11–14 (1984).

14. *See* Gerard V. Bradley, Church-State Relationships in America 48 (1987).

15. *See* Borden, *supra* note 13, at 100; Noonan, *supra* note 5, at 172.

16. The controversial nature of the subject is reflected in a 1791 New Hampshire bill proposing that anyone "convicted of speaking disrespectfully of any part of the bible should have their tongues bored thro with a hot iron." After spirited discussion, the bill was narrowly defeated. Borden, *supra* note 13, at 32–33.

17. *Id.* at 101.

18. *Id.* at 31, 101–03.

19. *See* Robert L. Cord, "Founding Intentions and the Establishment

Clause: Harmonizing Accommodation and Separation," 10 Harv. J.L. & Pub. Pol'y 47, 49 (1987).

20. Borden, *supra* note 13, at 103.

21. Bradley, *supra* note 14, at 21.

22. The discussion here has described differences regarding particular practices such as oath and Sabbath requirements. For a discussion detailing differences in general positions regarding free exercise issues, see Philip A. Hamburger, "A Constitutional Right of Religious Exemption: An Historical Perspective," 60 Geo. Wash. L. Rev. 915, 921–26 (1992). Hamburger argues that American opinion about free exercise issues comprised three main and conflicting positions, and he shows that differences among these positions could be very controversial when, on a state level, citizens attempted to codify a substantive free exercise right.

23. *See* Michael W. McConnell, "The Origins and Historical Understanding of the Free Exercise of Religion," 103 Harv. L. Rev. 1409, 1481 (1990).

24. *See* Hamburger, *supra* note 22, at 928 n. 59. ("The surviving debates about the Free Exercise Clause are remarkable chiefly for their meagerness.").

25. For a description of such a controversy in the state of New York, see *id.* at 924–26.

26. *Id.* at 1485 & n. 384.

27. It is this kind of difficulty that provokes advocates to resort to something like the singular conception of religious freedom discussed in chapter 1. If religious freedom can be contained in a singular principle or unitary ideal, then contemporary advocates can claim that their own positions follow from the "principle" of religious freedom even though eighteenth-century Americans may have (mis)understood that principle differently than the modern advocate understands it. I argued in chapter 1 that the singular conception of religious freedom is not plausible. And I would suggest that the divided state of opinion in the early constitutional period underscores that implausibility: There simply was (and is) no single or unitary "free exercise principle."

28. McConnell, *supra* note 23, at 1456–58. The various state provisions are collected in Arlin M. Adams & Charles J. Emmerich, A Nation Dedicated to Religious Liberty 115–21 (1990).

29. *Cf.* Borden, *supra* note 13, at 8 ("From 1776 on, conflicts over religious liberty — its definition, extent, and precise application — agitated society in many states.").

30. *See* Ellis Sandoz, A Government of Laws: Political Theory, Religion, and the American Founding 167 (1990) ("Liberty and license were poles apart to the founding generation. . . . ").

31. *See* Hamburger, *supra* note 22, at 917–18.

32. Curry, *supra* note 8, at 166.

33. For a discussion of Augustine's views on conscience, see David A.J. Richards, Toleration and the Constitution 86–88 (1986). Richards argues that although Augustine's theory of the soul entailed respect for conscience,

> resistance to the authority of the Church by schismatic Christians, such as the Donatists, appeared to Augustine so irrational that he came to see the resistance of the Donatists as the product not of reasonable disagreement, but of the culpable and vincible ignorance of persons who know the truth but who wilfully deny it through a corruption of the will.

Id. at 87–88.

34. *See* Titus 3:10–11 ("A man that is a heretic, after the first and second admonition, reject; knowing that he that is such is subverted, and sinneth, being condemned of himself.").

35. Cotton asserted:

> Fundamentals are so cleare, that a man cannot but be convinced in Conscience of the Truth of them after two or three Admonitions: and that therefore such a Person as still continues obstinate, is condemned of himselfe: and if he then be punished, He is not punished for his Conscience, but for sinning against his owne Conscience.

Quoted in McConnell, *supra* note 23, at 1422.

36. Bernard Bailyn, The Ideological Origins of the American Revolution 269 (1967).

37. Curry, *supra* note 8, at 219.

38. The Maryland Constitution, for example, recognized the religious liberty of "all persons, professing the Christian religion . . . unless, under colour of religion, any man shall disturb the good order, peace or safety of the State, or shall infringe the laws of morality, or injure others, in their natural, civil, or religious rights. . . . " *Quoted in* Adams & Emmerich, *supra* note 28, at 117.

39. *See* Noonan, *supra* note 5, at 174.

40. *See* James M. Washington, "The Crisis in the Sanctity of Conscience in American Jurisprudence," 42 DePaul L. Rev. 11, 21–22 (1992) ("In 1791 most political and ecclesiastical leaders in the Anglo-American world assumed that 'the rights of conscience' were natural and inalienable. But this did not forestall nearly 150 years of theological and philosophical debates about the meaning of this phrase."). Nor are those debates over; defining the concept of "freedom of conscience" remains difficult today. *See* Rodney K. Smith, "Conscience, Coercion, and the Establishment of Religion: The Beginning of an End to the Wandering of a Wayward Judiciary?," 43 Case W. Res. L. Rev. 917, 935–51 (1993).

41. For a helpful discussion of the very limited scope of state "free exercise" provisions, see Hamburger, *supra* note 22, at 932–36.

42. Northwest Ordinance art. 1, *reprinted in* 1 Documents of American Constitutional and Legal History 85, 88 (Melvin I. Urofsky ed., 1989).

43. Jay A. Barnett, Evolution of the Ordinance of 1787, at 60 (1891).

44. Paul Finkleman, "Slavery and Bondage in the 'Empire of Liberty,'" *in* The Northwest Ordinance: Essays on Its Formulation, Provisions, and Legacy 61, 67 (Frederick D. Williams ed., 1989) [hereinafter Northwest Ordinance].

45. *See* Gordon T. Stewart, "The Northwest Ordinance and the Balance of Power in North America," *in* Northwest Ordinance, *supra* note 44, at 21, 22–24, 33.

46. Finkleman, *supra* note 44, at 67.

47. *See* James Madison, "Memorial and Remonstrance Against Religious Assessments," *reprinted in* The Supreme Court on Church and State 18, 22–23 (Robert S. Alley ed., 1988).

48. Ruth H. Bloch, "Battling Infidelity, Heathenism, and Licentiousness: New England Missions and the Post-Revolutionary Frontier, 1792–1805," *in* Northwest Ordinance, *supra* note 44, at 39, 40–41.

49. *Id.* at 54–55.

50. *See generally* Sidney E. Mead, The Lively Experiment: The Shaping of Christianity in America 60 (1963).

51. Curry, *supra* note 8, at 202.

52. Akhil Amar appears to take this view. *See* text accompanying *supra* note 2. *Cf.* Stephen Pepper, "Taking the Free Exercise Clause Seriously," 1986 B.Y.U. L. Rev. 299, 300 ("The text of the free exercise clause is singularly absolute.").

Chapter 4

1. *See* Philip B. Kurland, "The Origins of the Religion Clauses of the Constitution," 27 Wm. & Mary L. Rev. 839, 842 (1986) (criticizing "'law office history,' written the way brief writers write briefs, by picking and choosing statements and events favorable to the client's cause").

2. *See, e.g.,* Mary Ann Glendon & Raul F. Yanes, "Structural Free Exercise," 90 Mich. L. Rev. 477, 541 (1991); Robert C. Palmer, "Akhil Amar: Elitist Populist and Anti-Textual Textualist," 16 S. Ill. U. L.J. 397, 400 (1992); William C. Porth & Robert P. George, "Trimming the Ivy: A Bicentennial Reexamination of the Establishment Clause," 90 W. Va. L. Rev. 109, 135–38 (1987); Note, "Rethinking the Incorporation of the Establishment Clause," 105 Harv. L. Rev. 1700, 1707 (1992) [hereinafter Harvard Note].

3. *See* arguments and sources discussed in Lee v. Weisman, 112 S. Ct. 2649, 2669 n. 2 (1992) (Souter, J., concurring).

4. 330 U.S. 1, 11–13 (1947).

5. For a more recent instance, see Edward P. Foley, "Political Liberalism and Establishment Clause Jurisprudence," 43 Case W. Res. L. Rev. 963, 980–81 (1993). Arguing that the establishment clause should be understood to have the same meaning as Madison's "Memorial and Remonstrance," Foley explains simply that Madison was the "principal author" of the clause, and he asserts without argument or evidence that Madison understood the establishment clause to have enacted his beliefs as expressed in "Memorial and Remonstrance."

6. For example, Mark Howe emphasized that the modern Supreme Court's imposition onto the establishment clause of Jefferson's notions about the proper relationship between church and state represented a distortion of history. Mark Dewolfe Howe, The Garden and the Wilderness 3–12 (1965).

7. *See, e.g.*, Daan Braveman, "The Establishment Clause and the Course of Religious Neutrality," 45 Md. L. Rev. 352, 373 (1986) (arguing that the "literal quest for the Framers' intent . . . [is] both futile and misdirected").

8. Donald L. Drakeman, Church-State Constitutional Issues 71–72 (1991).

9. *Id.* at 70.

10. *Id.* at 110.

11. *Id.*

12. *E.g.*, Daniel O. Conkle, "Toward a General Theory of the Establishment Clause," 82 Nw. U. L. Rev. 113, 1136–42 (1988); Harvard Note, *supra* note 2, at 1708–14; Philip B. Kurland, "The Irrelevance of the Constitution: The Religion Clauses of the First Amendment and the Supreme Court," 24 Vill. L. Rev. 3, 9–10 (1984); Joseph M. Snee, "Religious Disestablishment and the Fourteenth Amendment," 1954 Wash. U. L.Q. 371, 372 (describing incorporation of the establishment clause as a "constitutional *faux pas* as historic and embarrassing as *Swift v. Tyson*"). For a contrary view, see Palmer, *supra* note 2, at 398–400.

13. *Cf.* John F. Wilson, "Religion, Political Culture, and the Law," 41 DePaul L. Rev. 821, 835–36 (1992):

> This historically new role [for the religion clauses], which has become so familiar to us, is marvelously ironic. For the clauses that were crafted to keep Congress from interfering with the various expressions of regional hegemony in the states have become the basis for challenges to vestiges of that hegemony. . . . Thus, at one level of irony, the religion clauses . . . have become appropriated to specific purposes directly opposed to those that led to their adoption.

See also Drakeman, *supra* note 8, at 110–11 (arguing that incorporation "stood the framers' decision on its head").

14. *See, e.g.*, Conkle, *supra* note 12, at 1142.

15. Kurt T. Lash, The Second Adoption of the Free Exercise Clause:

Religious Exemptions Under the Fourteenth Amendment. Professor Lash's article has since been published in 88 Nw. U. L. Rev. 1106 (1994). My comments and quotations here, however, are based on the draft.

16. *Id.* at 1140 n. 157.

17. *See* Richard A. Posner, The Federal Courts: Crisis and Reform 286–87 (1985).

18. William E. Nelson, The Fourteenth Amendment: From Political Principle to Judicial Doctrine 3 (1988).

19. *See* Conkle, *supra* note 12, at 1137–39.

20. *Id.* at 1138 n. 124. Professor Lash points out that the Blaine Amendment was motivated by anti-Catholic sentiment and that it expressly protected the use of the Protestant Bible in schools. Lash, *supra* note 15, at 1147 n. 188. Lash may be right, but it is not clear how this observation is responsive to the evidence cited by Conkle and others.

21. Henry F. May, The Divided Heart: Essays on Protestantism and the Enlightenment in America 161–78 (1991).

22. *Id.* at 176–77.

23. Jon Butler, Awash in a Sea of Faith: Christianizing the American People 257–88 (1990).

24. *Id.* at 284.

25. *Id.* at 285–86.

26. Lash, *supra* note 15.

Chapter 5

1. Thus, Edward Foley argues that "the Constitution itself, properly understood, calls upon the judiciary to engage in the methodology of philosophy in order to perform the function of constitutional interpretation." Edward P. Foley, "Political Liberalism and Establishment Clause Jurisprudence," 43 Case W. Res. L. Rev. 963, 979 (1993). In this vein, after concluding that the establishment clause did not adopt any substantive principle or right of religious freedom, Daniel Conkle concludes that we must develop such a principle or right "on the basis of a theory of political-moral reasoning." Daniel O. Conkle, "Toward a General Theory of the Establishment Clause," 82 Nw. U. L. Rev. 1113, 1162 (1988). *See also* John Garvey, "Free Exercise and the Values of Religious Liberty," 18 Conn. L. Rev. 779, 783 (1986) (explaining need for a theory of religious freedom); Douglas Laycock, "Towards a General Theory of the Religion Clauses: The Case of Church Labor Relations and the Right to Church Autonomy," 81 Colum. L. Rev. 1373 (1981).

2. Harold J. Berman, Law and Revolution: The Formation of the Western Legal Tradition 9 (1983).

3. *See, e.g.*, Keekok Lee, The Positivist Science of Law (1989). For a discussion of this theme in American legal thought, see Grant Gilmore, The Ages of American Law 42–56, 99–101 (1977).

4. For a helpful overview of the Legal Realist movement, see William Twining, Karl Llewellyn and the Realist Movement (1973).

5. Bruce A. Ackerman, "Law and the Modern Mind by Jerome Frank," 103 Daedalus 119, 125 (1974).

6. Bruce A. Ackerman, Private Property and the Constitution (1977).

7. Bruce A. Ackerman, Social Justice in the Liberal State (1980); Bruce A. Ackerman, We the People: Foundations (1991).

8. The term and, to some degree, the issue were given currency by Alexander M. Bickel's classic, The Least Dangerous Branch (1962).

9. *See, e.g., id.* at 23–28; Robert H. Bork, The Tempting of America 143–60 (1990); Ronald Dworkin, A Matter of Principle 33–71 (1985); Herbert Wechsler, "Toward Neutral Principles of Constitutional Law," 73 Harv. L. Rev. 1 (1959).

10. Because the displacement of traditional legal authorities and techniques by political and economic theory is so pervasive in modern legal scholarship, familiarity may serve to deflect a fundamental question about how theory gets engrafted onto the Constitution. The question is nonetheless critical: Even if we could demonstrate that a particular theory of religious freedom (or free speech, or equality, or anything else) is the most plausible or attractive theory available, why does it follow that this theory is thereby part of the Constitution and hence enforceable by courts to invalidate laws that diverge from the theory?

My own view is that judges and scholars rely heavily, if implicitly, on the unitary conception of religious freedom discussed in chapter 1 (or on similar conceptions of free speech or equality or whatever) in order to connect their theories with the constitutional text. In other words, if it is assumed that the Constitution adopted "*the* principle of religious freedom" and if theorizing is about the "principle," then theory automatically has constitutional authority. Conversely, if the singular conception of religious freedom is untenable, then the connection between theory and the Constitution remains very problematic.

Important though this issue is, however, I intend to bypass it here in favor of an argument more directly focused on religious freedom. More specifically, I will try to show that there is not and cannot be any adequate general theory of religious freedom. Hence, even if good theories somehow deserve constitutional status, there is not in this area any good theory.

11. In his later writing, Alexander Bickel emphasized the shortcomings of and the obstacles to the use of "theory" in dealing with legal and political issues. *See, e.g.,* Alexander M. Bickel, The Morality of Consent 19–30 (1975).

12. *See, e.g.,* "Symposium: The Renaissance of Pragmatism in American Legal Thought," 63 S. Cal. L. Rev. 1569 (1990).

13. Thomas C. Grey, "Hear the Other Side: Wallace Stevens and Pragmatist Legal Theory," 63 S. Cal. L. Rev. 1569, 1569 (1990).

14. *See, e.g.*, Steven D. Smith, "Symbols, Perceptions, and Doctrinal Illusions: Establishment Neutrality and the 'No Endorsement' Test," 86 Mich. L. Rev. 266 (1987).

15. Steven D. Smith, "The Pursuit of Pragmatism," 100 Yale L.J. 409 (1990).

Chapter 6

1. *Cf.* John Mansfield, "The Religion Clauses of the First Amendment and the Philosophy of the Constitution," 72 Cal. L. Rev. 846, 848 (1984) (suggesting that religion clauses must be understood in light of "a philosophy of the Constitution regarding human nature, human destiny and other realities"). *See also* Gerard V. Bradley, "Church Autonomy in the Constitutional Order: The End of Church and State," 49 La. L. Rev. 1057, 1077 (1989) (arguing that "what we call 'church-state' arises and can only be discussed within an intellectual field that presupposes religious, particularly Christian concepts").

2. John Locke, "A Letter Concerning Toleration," *in* John Locke on Politics and Education 21, 24 (Classics Club ed., 1947).

3. *Id.* at 25.

4. *Id.* at 26.

5. *Id.* at 38 ("There is only one of these which is the true way to eternal happiness: but in this great variety of ways that men follow, it is still doubted which is the right one.").

6. *Id.* at 63 ("It is not the diversity of opinions, which cannot be avoided, but the refusal of toleration to those that are of different opinions, which might have been granted, that has produced all the bustles and wars that have been in the Christian world upon account of religion.").

7. *See, e.g., id.* at 41:

> But after all, the principal consideration, and which absolutely determines this controversy, is this: although the magistrates's opinion in religion be sound, and the way that he appoints be truly evangelical, yet if I be not thoroughly persuaded thereof in my own mind, there will be no safety for me in following it. No way whatsoever that I shall walk in against the dictates of my conscience, will ever bring me to the mansions of the blessed. I may grow rich by an art that I take not delight in; I may be cured of some disease by remedies that I have not faith in; but I cannot be saved by a religion that I distrust, and by a worship that I abhor. It is in vain for an unbeliever to take up the outward show of another man's profession. Faith only, and inward sincerity, are the things that procure acceptance with God.

8. *Id.* at 35.

9. "Moral actions belong therefore to the jurisdiction both of the out-

ward and inward court; . . . I mean, both of the magistrate and conscience." *Id.* at 52–53.

10. *Id.* at 57–58.

11. *Id.* at 58.

12. *See, e.g.*, Leo Pfeffer, Church, State, and Freedom 91 (1953)
("Locke himself did not pursue his ideas to their logical conclusion. . . .
The logical extension of his ideas was, however, effected by Jefferson,
Madison, and others responsible for the American experiment.").

13. *Id.* at 43.

14. *Id.* at 22–23, 38; *see* Timothy L. Hall, "Roger Williams and the
Foundations of Religious Liberty," 71 B.U. L. Rev. 455, 494 (1991) (footnote omitted): "Locke . . . tended to view questions of morality as significantly more important than those relating to religious doctrine and exercise. Thus, he protected doctrine and worship by marginalizing them. In
the overall scheme, such matters were not worthy of coercion because they
were not important."

15. Locke, *supra* note 2, at 25.

16. *Id.* at 37.

17. *Id.* at 49.

18. *See id.* at 27: "It is only light and evidence that can work a change
in men's opinions; and that light can in no manner proceed from corporal
sufferings, or any other outward penalties." *See generally id.* at 26–27.

19. *See, e.g.*, A. James Reichley, Religion in American Public Life
168–339 (1985).

20. *See generally* 2 Sidney Ahlstrom, A Religious History of the American People 250–73 (1975).

21. Augustine, "The Correction of the Donatists," *partially reprinted in*
John T. Noonan, Jr., The Believer and the Powers That Are 19, 20
(1987).

22. *Cf.* Hall, *supra* note 14, at 494 n.212 ("To the extent that we
import Locke's thinking about toleration into contemporary analysis without recognizing his underlying vision of religion, we risk appropriating a
theoretical construct inappropriate for an age less limited in its understanding of religious diversity than Locke's.").

23. Thus, Timothy Hall says, in a critical tone, that "the main differences between [Roger] Williams and Jefferson arose out of Jefferson's
notions about the nature of true religion, his impatience with, even intolerance of, religious views different from his own, and his apparent willing-
ness to let his own religious ideas define the scope of other people's religious
liberty." *Id.* at 505. If the analysis of this chapter is correct, then Hall is
descriptively accurate with respect to Jefferson, but he is wrong to suggest
that he has detected a distinctive feature in Jefferson's view. On the contrary, *everyone's* position on issues of religious freedom will arise out of
personal beliefs about, among other things, the nature of true religion.

24. The dependency of theory creates other obstacles that are not the

focus of this chapter. For example, background beliefs are likely to be transitory. This fact casts doubt on the efficacy of the practice of drawing from a variety of theories and rationales formulated at different times and places in an effort to construct a general theory of religious freedom. Insofar as the background beliefs on which earlier theories were based have been rejected, it is not clear why current thinkers or judges should be entitled to draw on those theories for support. For example, Locke's rationale for religious tolerance — and, following Locke, Jefferson's views about religious freedom — rested heavily on a minimalist conception of the proper functions of the state. That minimalist conception hardly commands a consensus today. Hence, it is unclear why current judges or legal scholars should feel entitled to invoke Locke's or Jefferson's *conclusions* about religious freedom when they reject the *premises* from which those conclusions were derived.

25. Michael McConnell approvingly describes the premise that underlies most modern religion clause scholarship:

> Let there be no doubt: The Establishment Clause was a deliberate choice to allow all sects and modes of belief, religious as well as secular, to compete for the allegiance of the people, *without official preference*. The attempt to press the Religion Clauses into service as an instrument for "collective relativism," or any other official orthodoxy, must be condemned in the strongest possible terms.

Michael W. McConnell, "Accommodation of Religion: An Update and a Response to Critics," 60 Geo. Wash. L. Rev. 685, 740 (1992) (emphasis added).

26. Mark 8:36.

27. *Cf.* Reynolds v. United States, 98 U.S. 145 (1878).

28. *Cf.* Wisconsin v. Yoder, 406 U.S. 205 (1972).

29. *Cf.* Reynolds, 98 U.S. at 165–66.

30. *Cf.* John Stuart Mill, On Liberty 111–13 (Curtis V. Shields ed., 1956) (first published in 1859) (defending right of Mormons to practice polygamy while also condemning the practice).

31. In Wisconsin v. Yoder, 406 U.S. 205 (1972), the Supreme Court excused an Amish community from complying with aspects of a state compulsory education law but named Thoreau as an example of a secular objector who would not be entitled to a similar exemption. *Id.* at 216.

32. *Cf.* Paul Kauper, Religion and the Constitution 23–24 (1964) (discussing differences between Catholic and Protestant conceptions of religious liberty).

33. Kathleen Sullivan takes this position. *See* Kathleen M. Sullivan, "Religion and Liberal Democracy," 59 U. Chi. L. Rev. 195, 197–99 (1992). *See also* Kyron Huigens, "Science, Freedom of Conscience, and the Establishment Clause," 13 U. Puget Sound L. Rev. 65, 104 (1989).

34. Whether Kathleen Sullivan understands her position in this way

is unclear. She introduces her view that the Constitution commands a secular public order in a vaguely historical way—she sometimes uses the past tense, and she alludes to a social contract that was ostensibly made at some point in time—but offers no historical evidence to support her claim or to dispel the suspicion that her social contract, like other familiar social contracts, is a convenient historical fiction. Sullivan, *supra* note 33, at 197–99. Hence, when Sullivan asserts that the Constitution establishes a secular public order, I cannot confidently say whether she means (a) that the framers intended this, (b) that the Supreme Court has construed the religion clauses to mean this, (c) that Sullivan herself likes this view and therefore attributes it to the Constitution by employing a helpful fiction, or (d) something else.

35. *Cf.* Michael W. McConnell, Religious Freedom at a Crossroads, 59 U. Chi. L. Rev. 115, 190–91 (1992): "Some argue for a totally secular public sphere . . . on the ground that the First Amendment committed the United States to a certain public philosophy: a liberal, democratic, secular 'civil religion,'. . . . As an historical assertion about the meaning of the First Amendment, however, this position is plainly false."

36. *Cf.* Richard S. Myers, "The Supreme Court and the Privatization of Religion," 41 Cath. U. L. Rev. 19, 74 (1991) (arguing that "although secular rationalism is part of the American tradition, *privileging* that conception of rationality would do violence to the views of most Americans").

37. Frederick Schauer, Free Speech: A Philosophical Enquiry 113 (1982).

38. For a discussion of the argument that religious toleration is not religious freedom, see Steven D. Smith, "The Restoration of Tolerance," 78 Cal. L. Rev. 305, 309–11 (1990).

39. Thomas Paine, "The Rights of Man," *in* Reflections on the Revolution in France and the Rights of Man 267, 324 (1973).

40. Quoted in William Lee Miller, The First Liberty 4–5 (1986).

41. Philip B. Kurland, The Religion Clauses and the Burger Court, 34 Cath. U. L. Rev. 1, 3 (1984).

42. *Cf.* Michael W. McConnell, "Christ, Culture, and Courts: A Niebuhrian Examination of First Amendment Jurisprudence," 42 DePaul L. Rev. 191, 221 (1992) ("[T]o presuppose or impose a model [of church-state relations] can itself be seen as the establishment of the corresponding theological position. . . . [The justices] seem not to understand that their judgments reflect controversial ecclesiological presuppositions. . . . ").

43. Sullivan, *supra* note 33, at 198, 201, 205 (emphasis added).

44. *Id.* at 201 (emphasis added).

45. *Id.* at 211.

46. In popular conception, for example, the late medieval period is likely regarded as perhaps the most oppressively uniform, in religious matters, in Western history: A single church dominated central and western

Europe, and bishops and inquisitors joined with secular authorities to punish anyone who dared to deviate from the orthodoxy carefully defined by theologians and scholastic philosophers like Aquinas. In contrast to this popular conception, however, Alistair McGrath notes "the astonishing doctrinal diversity of the later fourteenth and fifteenth centuries" and argues that "there was potentially a remarkably broad spectrum of theological opinions current within the universities and religious orders of Europe on the eve of the Reformation. . . . " Alister McGrath, *The Intellectual Origins of the European Reformation* 14, 19 (1987). See *id.* at 9–31, 69–93.

Chapter 7

1. *See, e.g.*, Texas Monthly, Inc. v. Bullock, 109 S. Ct. 890, 898–99 (1989); Walz v. Tax Commission, 397 U.S. 664, 668–69 (1970); Abington School District v. Schempp, 375 U.S. 203, 214–26 (1963); Everson v. Board of Education, 330 U.S. 1, 18 (1947).

2. *See, e.g.*, Douglas Laycock, "Formal, Substantive, and Disaggregated Neutrality Toward Religion," 39 DePaul L. Rev. 993 (1990); Michael W. McConnell, "Neutrality Under the Religion Clauses," 81 Nw. U. L. Rev. 146 (1986); Wilbur Katz, Religion and American Constitutions 70–76 (1964); Philip B. Kurland, "Of Church and State and the Supreme Court," 29 U. Chi. L. Rev. 1 (1961).

3. Phillip E. Johnson, "Concepts and Compromise in First Amendment Doctrine," 72 Cal. L. Rev. 817, 818 (1984).

4. *See, e.g.*, John T. Valauri, "The Concept of Neutrality in Establishment Clause Doctrine," 48 U. Pitt. L. Rev. 83 (1986). I have discussed the problem in "The Restoration of Tolerance," 78 Cal. L. Rev. 305 (1990), and in "Symbols, Perceptions, and Doctrinal Illusions: Establishment Neutrality and the 'No Endorsement' Test," 86 Mich. L. Rev. 266, 313–32 (1987). Michael McConnell invokes "feminist legal studies, critical legal studies, critical race studies and other postmodernist jurisprudence" in support of his contention that "[i]t is no longer intellectually credible to maintain that secular liberalism is simply the 'neutral' position." Michael W. McConnell, "Religious Freedom at a Crossroads," 59 U. Chi. L. Rev. 115, 134 (1992).

5. Board of Education v. Allen, 392 U.S. 236, 249 (1968) (Harlan, J., concurring).

6. *Cf.* Donald Beschle, "The Conservative as Liberal: The Religion Clauses, Liberal Neutrality, and the Approach of Justice O'Connor," 62 Notre Dame L. Rev. 151, 174 (1987) (comparing establishment neutrality to that required of a "judge or umpire").

7. As this observation may suggest, the following discussion of "neutrality" parallels the argument about "equality" in Peter Westen, "The Empty Idea of Equality," 95 Harv. L. Rev. 537 (1982). The parallel is

only partial, however; the argument here will not suggest that neutrality is an "empty" or meaningless concept but only that the concept is parasitic on more substantive values or theory.

8. The Supreme Court adopted this view in Sherbert v. Verner, 374 U.S. 398 (1963).

9. Considering a case in which a church is denied a public monetary award for which it would have been eligible except for its religious character, William Marshall criticizes the objection that "assumes that awards to secular organizations should be treated similarly to religious organizations. The failure to give the award to the church is a penalty only if one assumes that churches and other religious entities are to be treated similarly to nonreligious organizations." William P. Marshall, "Towards a Nonunifying Theory of Unconstitutional Conditions: The Example of the Religion Clauses," 26 San Diego L. Rev. 243, 248 (1989).

10. *See* Laycock, *supra* note 2.

11. *Id.* at 1001.

12. *Id.* at 1002.

13. "I mean that religion is to be left as wholly to private choice as anything can be." *Id.* What this would mean in the context of, say, state-supported compulsory education is highly problematic.

14. *See, e.g.*, Michael E. Smith, "The Special Place of Religion in the Constitution," 1983 Sup. Ct. Rev. 83, 112 (describing Alexander Bickel's view that religion is something that we are "bound to suffer" but should strive to replace).

15. *See, e.g.*, Gerard V. Bradley, "Protecting Religious Liberty: Judicial and Legislative Responsibilities," 42 DePaul L. Rev. 253, 260–61 (1992) ("Religion is, and should be acknowledged as, a basic human good. Government ought to promote it.").

16. John Locke, "A Letter Concerning Toleration," *in* John Locke on Politics and Education 21, 26 (Classic Club ed., 1947):

> [T]he magistrate may make use of arguments, and thereby draw the heterodox into the way of truth, and procure their salvation. . . . Magistracy does not oblige him to put off either humanity or Christianity; but it is one thing to persuade, another to command; one thing to press with arguments, another with penalties.

17. *See* Lemon v. Kurtzman, 403 U.S. 602, 618 (1971). The Court derived the "secular purpose and effect" prongs from Abington School District v. Schempp, 374 U.S. 203 (1963), which had justified these requirements as an application of government's obligation of religious neutrality.

18. *See, e.g.*, Abington School District v. Schempp, 374 U.S. 203, 225 (1963).

19. *See, e.g.*, Epperson v. Arkansas, 393 U.S. 97, 106 (1969):

While study of religions and of the Bible from a literary and historic viewpoint, presented objectively as part of a secular program of education, need not collide with the First Amendment's prohibition, the State may not adopt programs or practices in its public schools or colleges which 'aid or oppose' any religion. . . . This prohibition is absolute.

20. *See, e.g.*, Stanley Hauerwas & Michael Baxter, "The Kingship of Christ: Why Freedom of Belief Is Not Enough," 42 DePaul L. Rev. 107, 122–23 (1992) (discussing with approval Pius XI's "antipathy . . . for secular theory" and his view that "'secularism' has become a plague on modern politics, an 'evil spirit'") (footnotes omitted).

21. *Cf.* McConnell, *supra* note 4, at 189 ("The problem with the secularization baseline is that it is not neutral in any realistic sense.").

22. 393 U.S. 97 (1968).

23. *Id.* at 103–04.

24. *Id.* 106 (emphasis added) (citation omitted).

25. *Id.* at 107–09.

26. This characterization is open to debate insofar as it equates "not opposing" with "aiding."

27. The *Epperson* majority argued that this had been the motive that produced the antievolution law. 393 U.S. at 107–09.

28. *See* Justice Hugo L. Black's concurring opinion. *Id.* at 112–13.

29. While rejecting creationism as the product of "shoddy analysis of shaky data," Stephen Carter also points out that

[p]arents who want scientific creationism taught in schools do not share the view that they are asking the schools to teacher their religious beliefs. Their view is that they are asking the schools to teach the truth—not the moral truth with which religion is commonly associated in our dialogue, but a truth about the material world.

Stephen L. Carter, "The Separation of Church and Self," 46 SMU L. Rev. 585, 593–94 (1992).

30. This characterization is probably too charitable to the justices in the *Epperson* majority. The majority opinion contains two gratuitous footnotes that serve no apparent purpose except to ridicule Christian fundamentalists. 393 U.S. at 102 nn. 9 & 10. Thus, despite its insistence on "absolute" neutrality, the *Epperson* majority was not averse to expressing, or at least making rhetorical use of, contempt for fundamentalists.

31. For a helpful elaboration of this point, see Larry Alexander, "Liberalism, Religion, and the Unity of Epistemology," 30 San Diego L. Rev. 763 (1993).

32. *See* Elizabeth C. Nordbeck, Thunder on the Right: Understanding Conservative Christianity 12 (1990) (fundamentalists "stress the supernatural origins of the 'inherent' scriptures").

33. Suzanna Sherry, "Outlaw Blues," 87 Mich. L. Rev. 1418, 1427 (1989).

34. *Cf.* Stephen L. Carter, "The Inaugural Development Fund Lectures: Scientific Liberalism, Scientist Law," 69 Or. L. Rev. 471, 497 (1990) ("Faith-based epistemologies are not merely suspect when offered in debate; they are practically outlaws.").

35. *See* Stanley Ingber, "Religion or Ideology: A Needed Clarification of the Religion Clauses," 41 Stan. L. Rev. 233, 311–15 (1989); Gail Merel, "The Protection of Individual Choice: A Consistent Understanding of Religion Under the First Amendment," 45 U. Chi. L. Rev. 805, 813 (1978).

36. 753 F.2d 1528, 1535 (9th Cir. 1985) (Canby, J., concurring).

37. *Id.*

38. *Id.* at 1536.

39. *Id.* at 1541.

40. *Id.* at 1541 n. 25.

41. *Id.* at 1536 n. 6, 1538 n. 12.

42. *Cf.* Goldman v. Weinberger, 475 U.S. 503 (1986) (upholding, as against free exercise objection, military-dress regulation that precluded the wearing of a yarmulke).

43. Paul Tillich, A History of Christian Thought 310 (1967).

44. Discussing a related issue in a different case in which fundamentalists challenged part of the school curriculum, Nomi Maya Stolzenberg observes:

> Ultimately, the fundamentalists resisted the schools' mode because in "merely exposing" competing values and diverse ways of life, it implicitly teaches children that beliefs are matters of individual opinion; that values are the stuff of subjective thought; that religions are cultural systems which reflect the human hand of history; and that their doctrines are therefore open to debate. In so doing, the challenged educational program potentially estranges children from their parents' religious tradition and initiates them into the culture of modernity. . . .

Nomi Maya Stolzenberg, "'He Drew a Circle That Shut Me Out'; Assimilation, Indoctrination, and the Paradox of a Liberal Education," 106 Harv. L. Rev. 581, 659–60 (1993).

45. For example, the National Academy of Sciences has asserted, with specific reference to evolution, that "[r]eligion and science are separate and mutually exclusive realms of thought." *Quoted in* Phillip E. Johnson, Darwin on Trial 123–24 (1991). Of course, this "two-truth" position itself constitutes a rejection of a central element of the philosophy of a religious thinker like Thomas Aquinas. For a vivid description of the horror with which Aquinas regarded the two-truth theory, see G.K. Chesterton, Saint Thomas Aquinas 91–96 (1993).

46. For example, Phillip Johnson quotes William Provine, a critic of creationism and a historian of science at Cornell University, as asserting that "persons who manage to retain religious beliefs while accepting evolutionary biology 'have to check [their] brains at the church-house door.'" Johnson, *supra* note 45, at 124.

47. *Id.* at 129–31.

48. *See* Matt. 12:30; Luke 11:23; 1 John 2:15–17; Rev. 3:15–16.

49. H. Richard Niebuhr, Christ and Culture 45–82 (1951).

50. Malcolm Muggeridge, Jesus Rediscovered 100–05 (1969).

51. Kent Greenawalt, Religious Convictions and Political Choice 217 (1988).

52. David A.J. Richards, Toleration and the Constitution 140–41, 249–52 (1986).

53. *Id.* at 245.

54. *Id.*

55. *Id.* at 246.

56. Edward Foley, while arguing for this sort of common denominator approach, also concedes that the supposed common denominator of "public reason" is not shared by many citizens. Invoking John Rawls's concept of "public reason" based on an "overlapping consensus," Foley contends that government must be neutral toward all religions that join in this consensus; but government cannot be neutral toward religions that do not share the "consensus." Edward P. Foley, "Political Liberalism and Establishment Clause Jurisprudence," 43 Case W. Res. L. Rev. 963 (1993). Thus, liberalism properly and necessarily "discriminates against all those religions (and other belief-systems) that are inconsistent with liberalism." *Id.* at 966. Foley is more candid than most proponents of this view in acknowledging that this position of incomplete "neutrality" not only disfavors "illiberal" religions and beliefs but also necessarily rejects their theological views. *Id.* at 973–78. This candor is admirable, but it raises awkward questions: How can Foley continue to talk of an "overlapping consensus" that by his own analysis many citizens do not share? And how can he continue to defend the view that government must not endorse religion on the ground that disparaging any citizen's beliefs treats that citizen as less than equal, when by his own admission the "liberal" and "neutral" position he favors disparages the beliefs of potentially large numbers of citizens?

57. For a similar analysis, see Michael J. Perry, Love and Power: The Role of Religion and Morality in American Politics 8–28 (1991).

58. McConnell, *supra* note 2, at 162. *See also* William R. Marty, "To Favor Neither Religion Nor Nonreligion: Schools in a Pluralist Society," *in* Equal Separation: Understanding the Religion Clauses of the First Amendment 95, 97 (Paul J. Weber ed., 1990) (arguing that "[f]ar from being neutral, what is taught in a secularized public school is an 'implicit denigration of religion'"); Alan Schwarz, "The Non-Establishment Principle: A

Reply to Professor Gianella," 81 Harv. L. Rev. 1465, 1477 (1968) (critic-izing the "anti-religionism of the public schools"). For an excellent discus-sion describing and in some respects supporting the claims that secular public education is hostile to some kinds of religion, see George W. Dent, Jr., "Religious Children, Secular Schools," 61 S. Cal. L. Rev. 863 (1988).

59. William P. Marshall, "'We Know It When We See It': The Su-preme Court and Establishment," 59 S. Cal. L. Rev. 495, 498 (1984) (emphasis added).

60. *Id.* at 513.

61. 465 U.S. 668, 688–92 (1984) (O'Connor, J., concurring).

62. 492 U.S. 573 (1989).

63. *See, e.g.*, sources cited in Steven D. Smith, "Symbols, Perceptions, and Doctrinal Illusions: Establishment Neutrality and the 'No Endorse-ment' Test," 86 Mich. L. Rev. 266, 274 n. 45 (1987).

64. *See, e.g.*, A.J. Ayer, The Foundations of Empirical Knowledge (1940); Bertrand Russell, Our Knowledge of the External World 75–134 (2d ed. 1929).

65. For example, Ayer contended that a sense-datum proposition is "incorrigible," or incapable of being falsified, because it is "completely veri-fied by the existence of the sense-datum which it describes; and so it is inferred that to doubt the truth of such a proposition is not merely irrational but meaningless." Ayer, *supra* note 64, at 83.

66. H.H. Price expressed the argument in this way:

> When I see a tomato there is much that I can doubt. I can doubt whether it is a tomato that I am seeing, and not a cleverly painted piece of wax. I can doubt whether there is any material thing there at all. Perhaps what I took for a tomato was really a reflection; perhaps I am even the victim of some hallucination. One thing however I cannot doubt: that there exists a red patch of a round and somewhat bulgy shape, standing out from a back-ground of other colour-patches, and having a certain visual depth, and that this whole field of colour is directly present to my consciousness. What the red patch is, whether a substance, or a state of a substance, or an event, whether it is physical or psychi-cal or neither, are questions that we may doubt about. But that something is red and round then and there I cannot doubt. Whether the something persists even for a moment before and after it is present to my consciousness, whether other minds can be conscious of it as well as I, may be doubted. But that it now *exists*, and that *I* am conscious of it—by me at least who am conscious of it this cannot possibly be doubted.

H.H. Price, Perception 3 (rev. ed. 1950).

67. J.L. Austin, Sense and Sensibilia 113 (1962) (emphasis added).

68. 330 U.S. at 58–60 (Rutledge, J., dissenting).

69. *Id.* at 18 (majority opinion).

70. For a similar analysis, see Valauri, *supra* note 4, at 94–96.

71. *Cf.* Foley, *supra* note 56 (arguing that government should be neutral toward religion even though complete neutrality is impossible).

72. *See, e.g.*, Robert L. Cord, Separation of Church and State: Historical Fact and Current Fiction 161–65 (1982).

73. *See* 1 Sidney Ahlstrom, A Religious History of the American People 573 (1975).

74. *See, e.g.*, James D. Gordon III, "Free Exercise on the Mountaintop," 79 Cal. L. Rev. 91, 110 (1991) ("The right to practice one's religion should not be reduced to a question of political influence, completely subject to the whims of transient and shifting majorities.") (footnotes omitted).

75. The marginalization of religious minorities in this usage of the concept of neutrality is even more marked when a writer *does* concede their existence but continues to treat them as insignificant in making judgments about neutrality. *See, e.g.*, Cord, *supra* note 72, at 80 ("Nor does the appropriation of federal monies to Christian schools indicate discriminatory aid to religion, for . . . the numbers of professed non-Christians were minute in the early years of the Federal Republic.").

76. *Cf.* Charles Taylor, "The Politics of Recognition," *in* Multiculturalism and "The Politics of Recognition" 25, 63 (Amy Gutman ed., 1992) (ascribing to "liberal neutrality" the "marginalization of segments of [liberal societies'] populations that stem from other cultures").

77. Once again, Edward Foley's discussion of neutrality seems a remarkably candid acknowledgment of this consequence. As noted, Foley argues that the state is required to be "neutral" and that this very requirement means that the state must "discriminate [] against all those religions (and other belief systems) that are inconsistent with liberalism." *See supra* note 56, at 966.

78. *See, e.g.*, Richard J. Bernstein, Beyond Objectivism and Relativism 230 (1985) (noting the "growing sense that there may be nothing — not God, Philosophy, Science, or Poetry — that satisfies our longing for ultimate foundations, for a fixed Archimedean point upon which we can secure our thought and action").

79. *See, e.g.*, Hilary Putnam, Reason, Truth, and History 74 (1981) (suggesting that "we are left without the God's Eye View"); *id.* at 64 ("Saying that something is red, or warm, or furry, is saying that it is so-and-so *in relation to us*, not how it is from a God's Eye point of view.").

Chapter 8

1. This appears to be the course taken by Kathleen Sullivan. *See* Kathleen M. Sullivan, "Religion and Liberal Democracy," 59 U. Chi. L.

Rev. 195, 197–201 (1992). *See also* Kyron Huigens, "Science, Freedom of Conscience, and the Establishment Clause," 13 U. Puget Sound L. Rev. 65, 104 (1989) (arguing that the Constitution "does not embody an ideal of neutrality between religion and non-religion. On the contrary, the Constitution positively favors the secular.").

2. *See, e.g.*, Bruce A. Ackerman, We the People: Foundations 160 (1991). Edward Gaffney points out that "among academics [there] seems to be an uncritical sociological assumption that America is a firmly secular nation." Edward Gaffney, "Hostility to Religion, American Style," 42 DePaul L. Rev. 263, 268 (1992).

3. Martin E. Marty, "The Sacred and Secular in American History," *in* Transforming Faith: The Sacred and Secular in Modern American History 1, 8 (M.L. Bradbury & James B. Gilbert eds., 1989).

4. *Cf.* Frederick Mark Gedicks & Roger Hendrix, "Democracy, Autonomy, and Values: Some Thoughts on Religion and Law in Modern America," 60 S. Cal. L. Rev. 1579, 1618 (1987):

> Much as those who influence American political and cultural institutions may want to insist that ours is a secular state . . . , Americans remain avowedly religious, with all of the unrational and unempirical — and spiritual and transcendent — conceptions of reality which that term implies. Insistence upon exclusively secular constructions of reality today is as undemocratic as social darwinism was in 1906.

5. I focus on *secular* approaches to religious freedom, not on *religious* approaches, because secular approaches are the kind taken in modern legal discourse, almost without exception. It is possible, of course, that a religious approach might produce an adequate theory of the proper relationship between church and state even if a secular approach cannot. But I doubt it. For a powerful argument to the contrary offered from an unapologetically religious perspective, see Stanley Hauerwas & Michael Baxter, "The Kingship of Christ: Why Freedom of Belief Is Not Enough," 42 DePaul L. Rev. 107 (1992). Hauerwas and Baxter conclude that "Christians are called first and foremost not to resolve the tension between church and state, but to acknowledge the Kingship of Christ in their lives, which means *leaving church-state relations profoundly unresolved*, until the day when He comes again in glory." *Id.* at 126 (emphasis added).

6. Even if this conclusion is correct, of course, it is possible that some other secular rationale might succeed where these common rationales fail. I do not pretend, therefore, to *demonstrate* the impossibility of a secular theory of religious freedom, but only to suggest the improbability that such a theory could be devised.

7. *See, e.g.*, Christopher F. Mooney, Public Virtue: Law and the Social Character of Religion 24–25 (1986).

8. Perhaps the most careful elaboration of this justification is Timothy

L. Hall, "Religion and Civic Virtue: A Justification of Free Exercise," 67 Tul. L. Rev. 87 (1992). *See also* Michael W. McConnell, "Accommodation of Religion," 1985 Sup. Ct. Rev. 1, 16–19; Alan Schwarz, "No Imposition of Religion: The Establishment Clause Value," 77 Yale L.J. 692, 713 (1968).

9. 1 Alexis de Tocqueville, Democracy in America 316 (Francis Bowen trans., Phillips Bradley ed., 1945).

10. Gibbon's diagnosis of the way in which Christianity undermined civic virtue is worth quoting:

> The Christians were not less adverse to the business than to the pleasures of this world. The defence of our persons and property they knew not how to reconcile with the patient doctrine which enjoined an unlimited forgiveness of past injuries and commanded them to invite the repetition of fresh insults. Their simplicity was offended by the use of oaths, by the pomp of magistracy, and by the active contention of public life; nor could their humane ignorance be convinced that it was lawful on any occasion to shed the blood of our fellow-creatures, either by the sword of justice or by that of war, even though their criminal or hostile attempts should threaten the peace and safety of the whole community. It was acknowledged that, under a less perfect law, the powers of the Jewish constitution had been exercised with the approbation of Heaven by inspired prophets and by anointed kings. The Christians felt and confessed that such institutions might be necessary for the present system of the world, and they cheerfully submitted to the authority of their pagan governors. But while they inculcated the maxims of passive obedience, they refused to take any active part in the civil administration or the military defence of the empire. Some indulgence might perhaps be allowed to those persons who, before their conversion, were already engaged in such violent and sanguinary occupations; but it was impossible that the Christians, without renouncing a more sacred duty, could assume the character of soldiers, of magistrates, or of princes. This indolent or even criminal disregard to the public welfare exposed them to the contempt and reproaches of the pagans, who very frequently asked, What must be the fate of the empire, attacked on every side by the barbarians, if all mankind should adopt the pusillanimous sentiments of the new sect? To this insulting question the Christian apologists returned obscure and ambiguous answers, as they were unwilling to reveal the secret cause of their security — the expectation that before the conversion of mankind was accomplished war, government, the Roman empire, and the world itself would be no more. It may be observed that in this instance likewise the situation of the first Christians coincided very happily with their religious scruples,

and that their aversion to an active life contributed rather to excuse them from the service than to exclude them from the honours of the state and army.

1 Edward Gibbon, The History of the Decline and Fall of the Roman Empire 549–51 (H.H. Milman ed., 1845) (footnotes omitted).

11. Steven G. Gey, "Why is Religion Special?: Reconsidering the Accommodation of Religion Under the Religion Clauses of the First Amendment," 52 U. Pitt. L. Rev. 75, 178, 184 (1990). *See also* William P. Marshall, "The Other Side of Religion," 44 Hastings L.J. 843 (1993); Lynne Henderson, "Authoritarianism and the Rule of Law," 66 Ind. L.J. 379, 387 (1991) (suggesting that religion need not but is likely to produce authoritarianism); Stanley Ingber, "Religion or Ideology: A Needed Clarification of the Religion Clauses," 41 Stan. L. Rev. 233, 285 (1989) ("An essential incompatibility exists between the potential absolutism of religion and the individualistic premises of liberal political theory."); John Ladd, "Politics and Religion in America: The Enigma of Pluralism," *in* Religion, Morality, and the Law: Nomos 30 263, 275 (J. Roland Pennock & John W. Chapman eds., 1988) (suggesting that "the seeds of intolerance and perhaps of violence are embedded within the very concept of religious doctrine").

12. Michael E. Smith, "The Special Place of Religion in the Constitution," 1983 Sup. Ct. Rev. 83, 105–07. *See also* Michael W. McConnell, "Religious Freedom at a Crossroads," 59 U. Chi. L. Rev. 115, 120 (1992) (observing that during the Warren and Burger eras the "Court's opinions seemed to view religion as an unreasoned, aggressive, exclusionary, and divisive force").

13. *Cf.* Harvey Cox, "The Influence of Religion in America—More, Less, or What?," *in* An Unsettled Arena: Religion and the Bill of Rights 122–23 (Ronald C. White, Jr., & Albright G. Zimmerman eds., 1990) (describing and criticizing "the habit of speaking of 'religion' in the singular").

14. *See* West Virginia State Board of Education v. Barnette, 319 U.S. 624, 629 (1943).

15. The Articles of Faith of the Church of Jesus Christ of Latter-Day Saints, art. 12.

16. Mark V. Tushnet, "The Emerging Principle of Accommodation of Religion (Dubitante)," 76 Geo. L.J. 1691, 1696 (1988).

17. *See* Hall, *supra* note 8, at 89, 117–19.

18. Mass. Const. of 1780, art. 3, *reprinted in* The American Constitutions and Religion 40 (Conrad Henry Moehlman comp., 1938).

19. "A Bill Establishing a Provision for Teachers of the Christian Religion," *reprinted in* Robert L. Cord, Separation of Church and State: Historical Fact and Current Fiction 242 (1982).

20. *Cf.* Hauerwas & Baxter, *supra* note 5, at 115–20 (arguing that

religious freedom, as understood in this country, degenerates into religious indifferentism).

21. *See, e.g.*, Brown v. Board of Education, 347 U.S. 483, 493 (1954) ("Compulsory school attendance laws and the great expenditures for education both demonstrate our recognition of the importance of education to our democratic society. . . . It is the very foundation of good citizenship.").

22. *See, e.g.*, Michael Eric Dyson, "'God Almighty has Spoken from Washington, D.C.': American Society and Christian Faith," 42 DePaul L. Rev. 128, 136 (1992).

23. Tocqueville, *supra* note 9, at 322.

24. *Id.* at 323.

25. *Id.* at 325.

26. *Id.* at 322–23.

27. *See* Grand Rapids School District v. Ball, 473 U.S. 373, 389–92 (1985); Larkin v. Grendel's Den, 459 U.S. 116, 125–26 (1982).

28. For a cogent discussion of the error in simply importing a "no aid" conclusion from an era in which government was generally passive into an era in which government plays a vastly different role, see McConnell, *supra* note 12, at 183–86.

29. Michael Paulsen, "Religion, Equality, and the Constitution: An Equal Protection Approach to Establishment Clause Adjudication," 61 Notre Dame L. Rev. 311, 354–55 (1986).

30. *See* McConnell, *supra* note 12, at 132–33.

31. Thus, my discussion is not intended to contradict the analysis in Hall, *supra* note 8, most of which I find entirely plausible. My disagreement is only with Hall's claim that civic virtue considerations are adequate to permit one "to construct a *theory* of free exercise." *Id.* at 90 (emphasis added).

32. *See, e.g.*, Michael W. McConnell, "Political and Religious Disestablishment," 1986 B.Y.U. L. Rev. 405, 413 ("Religious differences in this country have never generated the civil discord experienced in political conflicts over such issues as the Vietnam War, racial segregation, the Red Scare, unionization, or slavery.").

33. *See* Ira C. Lupu, "Models of Church-State Interaction and the Strategy of the Religion Clauses," 42 DePaul L. Rev. 223, 229–33 (1992).

34. *See, e.g.*, Patricia U. Bonomi, Under the Cope of Heaven: Religion, Society, and Politics in Colonial America 14 (1986) ("Only through . . . [an established church], so the [colonial] leaders believed, might the colonists ward off the evils of religious strife. . . . "); Sidney E. Mead, The Lively Experiment: The Shaping of Christianity in America 60 (1963) ("For more than fourteen hundred years . . . it was a universal assumption that the stability of the social order and the safety of the state demanded the religious solidarity of all the people in one church.").

35. Even in this context, however, it would not follow that a "no aid"

principle is indicated; broadly "nonpreferential" aid to religion generally might be compatible with the peacekeeping purpose of the "no establishment" policy.

36. Peter Nicholson, "Toleration as a Moral Ideal," *in* Aspects of Toleration 164 (John Horton & Susan Mendus eds., 1985).

37. Michael J. Perry urges this point in Love and Power: The Role of Religion and Morality in American Politics 100, 132–33 (1991).

38. Steven Runciman, The Medieval Manichee 1 (1947).

39. Michael J. Sandel, "Freedom of Conscience or Freedom of Choice?," *in* Articles of Faith, Articles of Peace: The Religious Liberty Clauses and the American Public Philosophy 74, 86 (James Davison Hunter & Os Guiness eds., 1990).

40. *See* Leo Pfeffer, Religion, State, and the Burger Court 82–86 (1984) (describing outrage generated by the school-prayer decisions); John S. Baker, Jr., "The Religion Clauses Reconsidered: The *Jaffree* Case," 15 Cumb. L. Rev. 125, 139 (1984) ("The Supreme Court's school-prayer decisions have fanned, rather than doused, the flames of religious factionalism.").

41. *See, e.g.*, County of Allegheny v. ACLU, 109 S. Ct. 3086 (1989); Lynch v. Donnelly, 465 U.S. 668, 687–93 (1984) (O'Connor, J., concurring).

42. Justice John Marshall Harlan maintained, for example, that "[w]hat is at stake as a matter of policy is preventing that kind and degree of government involvement in religious life that, as history teaches us, is apt to lead to strife and frequently strain a political system to the breaking point." Walz v. Tax Commission, 397 U.S. 664, 694 (1970) (Harlan, J., concurring).

43. For characteristic expressions of this rationale, see, e.g., *Allegheny County*, 109 S. Ct. at 3102–03 (Blackmun, J.), at 3118–19 (O'Connor, J., concurring); Neal R. Feigenson, "Political Standing and Government Endorsement of Religion: An Alternative to Current Establishment Doctrine," 40 DePaul L. Rev. 53, 55 (1990). Probably the most careful and thoughtful development of this approach is Kenneth L. Karst, "The First Amendment, the Politics of Religion, and the Symbols of Government," 27 Harv. C.R.-C.L. L. Rev. 503 (1992).

44. *See* William P. Marshall, "The Concept of Offensiveness in Establishment and Free Exercise Clause Jurisprudence," 66 Ind. L.J. 351, 358–63 (1991).

45. *See* Alan E. Brownstein, "Harmonizing the Heavenly and Earthly Spheres: The Fragmentation and Synthesis of Religion, Equality, and Speech in the Constitution," 51 Ohio St. L.J. 89, 147 (1990).

46. *See* Everett C. Ladd, "Secular and Religion America," *in* Unsecular America 14, 28 (Richard J. Neuhaus ed., 1988) (survey evidence shows that the essential notion of separation of church and state is "universally accepted" by Americans).

47. *See* Carl Esbeck, "Religion and the Neutral State: Imperative or Impossibility?," 15 Cumb. L. Rev. 67, 77 (1984) (describing "theocentric" believers who hold that "a state, to be legitimate, must acknowledge that its authority to govern is from God").

48. *See* Richard S. Myers, "The Supreme Court and the Privatization of Religion," 41 Cath. U. L. Rev. 19, 50 (1991).

49. The Supreme Court invalidated such a statute in Edwards v. Aguillard, 482 U.S. 578 (1987).

50. *See* Daniel O. Conkle, "Toward a General Theory of the Establishment Clause," 82 Nw. U. L. Rev. 1113, 1174 n. 238 (1988) ("The teaching of evolution in the public schools . . . deeply offends the religious sensibilities of some. . . . ").

51. Wilbur Katz, Religion and American Constitutions 23–24 (1964).

52. 465 U.S. 668 (1984).

53. *See* William Van Alstyne, "Trends in the Supreme Court: Mr. Jefferson's Crumbling Wall — A Comment on *Lynch v. Donnelly*," 1984 Duke L.J. 770, 781 (decision showed "a paradigmatic disregard of the establishment clause in virtually every dimension of its concerns"); Daan Braveman, "The Establishment Clause and the Course of Religious Neutrality," 45 Md. L. Rev. 352, 353 (1986) (*Lynch* was "devastating to first amendment doctrine"); Douglas Laycock, "Equal Access and Moments of Silence: The Equal Status of Religious Speech by Private Speakers," 81 Nw. U. L. Rev. 1, 8 (1986) (*Lynch* was "wholly unprincipled and indefensible"); Norman Dorsen, "The United States Supreme Court: Trends and Prospects," 21 Harv. C.R.-C.L. L. Rev. 1, 22 (1986) (*Lynch* "marked the greatest incursion to date on the separation of church and state"); Philip Kurland, "The Religion Clauses and the Burger Court," 34 Cath. U. L. Rev. 1, 12–13 (1984) (*Lynch* was "disingenuous" and "sleazy"); Janet Dolgin, "Religious Symbols and the Establishment of a National Religion," 39 Mercer L. Rev. 495, 502 (1988) (comparing *Lynch* to *Plessy v. Ferguson*).

54. Pfeffer, *supra* note 40, at 124.

55. *Cf.* Phillip E. Johnson, "Concepts and Compromise in First Amendment Doctrine," 72 Cal. L. Rev. 817, 831 (1984) ("[B]y encouraging persons who are easily offended by religious symbolism to believe that the courts stand open to remedy their complaints, the courts foster divisive conflicts over religion.").

56. Marshall, *supra* note 44, at 375–76.

57. Laycock, *supra* note 53, at 8; Feigenson, *supra* note 43, at 98 n. 210. Feigenson also argues that the display of religious art in public galleries raises major constitutional issues. *Id.* at 109–10.

58. Although the justices have acknowledged that context is important in determining whether a symbol sends a religious message, *see, e.g., Allegheny County*, 109 S. Ct. at 3120–21 (O'Connor, J., concurring), once such a message has been detected, the Court has automatically invalidated the

challenged law or symbol. The Court has made no effort to determine whether *compelled elimination* of the symbol will produce more alienation than the symbol itself produces.

59. For a discussion of the problem of alienating religious citizens, see Frederick M. Gedicks, "Some Political Implications of Religious Belief," 4 Notre Dame J.L. Ethics & Pub. Pol'y 419, 432–39 (1990).

60. *See, e.g.*, Conkle, *supra* note 50, at 1177–79; Feigenson, *supra* note 43, at 82 n. 143, 112 (advocating requirement that government follow the "least alienating alternative"). Kenneth Karst appears to favor a similar approach. Karst, *supra* note 43, at 516.

61. Conkle, *supra* note 50, at 1177–79.

62. Although Conkle believes that messages offensive to "insiders" will produce less overall alienation, there appears to be no a priori reason to assume that this is true. Indeed, on the assumption that in a majoritarian system there are likely to be more "insiders" than "outsiders," we might suppose just the opposite to be true; messages hostile to "insiders" should usually produce more overall alienation, if only because there are more "insiders" who will take offense. The earlier hypothetical community about Baal-worshipers and Diana-worshipers reflects such a scenario. Given the difficulties in the real world both of measuring alienation and of categorizing citizens as "insiders" or "outsiders," however, any prediction in this regard must remain a matter of pure speculation.

63. Conkle, *supra* note 50, at 1178.

64. *See* R. Laurence Moore, Religious Outsiders and the Making of Americans 155–56 (1984) (describing the "perception of aloneness among evangelical Protestants"), 165 (noting "the outsider consciousness that developed among average American Protestants"). Since between 27 million and 40 million Americans may regard themselves as Fundamentalists or Evangelicals, moreover, *id.* at 167, the alienation felt by this group can hardly be dismissed as negligible.

65. *Cf.* Joel F. Carpenter, "From Fundamentalism to the New Evangelical Coalition," *in* Evangelicalism and Modern America 3, 9 (George Marsden ed., 1984) (exploring how in different senses Fundamentalists have regarded themselves as both "insiders" and "outsiders").

66. Indeed, the very concept of "alienation," or symbolic exclusion, is difficult to grasp. What exactly is "alienation"? How, if at all, does "alienation" differ from "anger," "annoyance," "frustration," or "disappointment" that every person who finds himself in a political minority is likely to feel? "Alienation" might refer to nothing more than an awareness by an individual that she belongs to a religious minority, accompanied by the realization that at least on some kinds of issues she is unlikely to be able to prevail in the political process. *Cf.* Mark V. Tushnet, "The Constitution of Religion," 18 Conn. L. Rev. 701, 712 (1986) ("[N]onadherents who believe that they are excluded from the political community are merely expressing the disappointment felt by everyone who has lost a fair fight in the arena of

politics."). That awareness may be discomforting. But is it the sort of phenomenon for which constitutional law can provide an efficacious remedy? Constitutional doctrine that stifles the message will not likely alter the reality — or a minority's awareness of that reality.

67. *Cf.* George W. Dent, Jr., "Religious Children, Secular Schools," 61 S. Cal. L. Rev. 863, 921–22 (1988) (arguing that whether removal of religiously offensive material from school curriculum will reduce strife presents a question "that courts are ill-equipped to handle" and that is better left to local school boards).

68. *See* Smith, *supra* note 12, at 96.

69. *See, e.g., id.* at 96, McConnell, *supra* note 32, at 413; Schwarz, *supra* note 8, at 710–11.

70. James L. Guth, "Secular Scholars and the Religious Right," The Chronicle of Higher Education, Apr. 7, 1993, at B3.

71. *See* Robert Wuthnow, The Struggle for America's Soul: Evangelicals, Liberals, and Secularism 55–57 (1989); Matthew C. Moen, The Christian Right and Congress 11–13 (1989); Ronald B. Flowers, "On Battling Over the Intentions and Morality of Nation's Founders," *in* The Lively Experiment Continued 160, 162–63 (J. Brauer ed., 1987).

72. Cox, *supra* note 13, at 115–16.

73. For an academic expression of this view, see David Louisell, "Does the Constitution Require a Purely Secular Society?," 26 Cath. U. L. Rev. 20 (1976).

74. Stephen L. Carter, "The Separation of Church and Self," 46 SMU L. Rev. 585, 600 (1992).

75. Gedicks, *supra* note 59, at 432.

Chapter 9

1. Mark Dewolfe Howe, The Garden and the Wilderness 65 (1965).

2. *Cf.* Michael W. McConnell, "Christ, Culture, and Courts: A Niebuhrian Examination of First Amendment Jurisprudence," 42 DePaul L. Rev. 191, 221 (1992): "How can the rights and duties of citizens be reconciled to the obligations and blessings of faith? In my view, within broad limits, the best answer is that given by Niebuhr: We must work it out for ourselves. The First Amendment does not answer the question for us."

3. Howe, *supra* note 1, at 8.

4. *See* Pierre Schlag, "Writing for Judges," 63 U. Colo. L. Rev. 419 (1992); Pierre Schlag, "Normativity and the Politics of Form," 139 U. Pa. L. Rev. 801 (1991).

5. This tendency to write prescriptively for courts is not universal; not surprisingly, some of the best scholarship in this area does *not* adopt this formula. Professor Howe's *The Garden and the Wilderness* is an excellent example.

6. *See, e.g.,* Ronald Dworkin, A Matter of Principle 33–71 (1985);

Alexander M. Bickel, The Least Dangerous Branch 23–28 (1962); Herbert Wechsler, "Toward Neutral Principles of Constitutional Law," 73 Harv. L. Rev. 1 (1959).

7. They might begin that inquiry by trying to clarify just what a "principle" is. As far as I can tell, nearly all judges and constitutional scholars talk freely about "principles" but without having any clear or satisfactory notion about what sort of thing a "principle" is, or what the ontological status of a "principle" might be. *See* Steven D. Smith, "Idolatry in Constitutional Interpretation," 79 Va. L. Rev. 583, 619–25 (1993).

8. Harold J. Berman, Faith and Order: The Reconciliation of Law and Religion 289 (1993).

9. *Id.* at 304 (footnote omitted).

10. For a brief but cogent discussion of these difficulties, see John Hart Ely, Democracy and Distrust 60–63 (1980).

11. For an important recent attempt to understand constitutional law as a distinctive kind of tradition, see H. Jefferson Powell, The Moral Tradition of American Constitutionalism (1993).

12. *See id.* at 83.

13. Henry P. Monaghan, "Foreword: Constitutional Common Law," 89 Harv. L. Rev. 1 (1975).

14. *Id.* at 3; *see id.* at 26–30.

15. I do not mean to imply that a tradition-based account of religious freedom is the only possible alternative to an account that distills religious freedom into a positivist or theoretical principle. It is also possible, for example, that modern difficulties in understanding, discussing, and protecting religious freedom derive from a deeply entrenched assumption accepting what one might call "the omnijurisdictional state," and hence that religious freedom might be understood in terms of revived, extraconstitutional limits on the state's jurisdiction.

16. *Id.* at 37. Of course, insofar as one church is officially established, that church *does* receive recognition and benefits unavailable to other churches, and if this preferential treatment itself is described as a violation of religious liberty, then religious freedom is diminished by definition. For a helpful assessment, see Susan M. Gilles, "'Worldly Corruptions' and 'Ecclesiastical Depredations': How Bad Is an Established Church?," 42 DePaul L. Rev. 349 (1992).

17. Arlin M. Adams & Charles J. Emmerich, A Nation Dedicated to Religious Liberty 32 (1990).

18. John T. Noonan, Jr., "The End of Free Exercise?," 42 DePaul L. Rev. 567, 568–70 (1992).

19. *Id.* at 575.

20. *See* Grand Rapids School District v. Ball, 473 U.S. 373 (1985); Aguilar v. Felton, 473 U.S. 402 (1985).

21. This point is emphasized in J. Woodford Howard, Jr., "The Robe and the Cloth: The Supreme Court and Religion in the United States," 7 J.L. & Pol. 481, 517–23 (1991).

22. *See* James D. Gordon III, "Free Exercise on the Mountaintop," 79 Cal. L. Rev. 91, 109–10 (1991); David C. Williams & Susan H. Williams, "Volitionalism and Religious Liberty," 76 Cornell L. Rev. 769, 895 (1991).

23. Neal Devins, "Fundamentalist Christian Educators v. State: An Inevitable Compromise," 60 Geo. Wash. L. Rev. 818, 822 (1992).

24. *Id.* at 820.

25. William Marshall observes that even before *Smith*, the Supreme Court gave very little free exercise protection to religion. William P. Marshall, "The Case Against the Constitutionally Compelled Free Exercise Exemption," 40 Case W. Res. L. Rev. 357, 366–72 (1990). *Cf.* Michael McConnell, "Free Exercise Revisionism and the *Smith* Decision," 57 U. Chi. L. Rev. 1109 (1990) (acknowledging that "the free exercise doctrine was more talk than substance").

26. The Supreme Court has given the federal statute requiring employers to accommodate the religious practices of their employees a very narrow reading, *see* TWA v. Hardison, 432 U.S. 65 (1977), and it has invalidated other legislatively granted accommodations on the ground that these accommodations advanced or endorsed religion, *see, e.g.*, Texas Monthly v. Bullock, 489 U.S. 1 (1989) (invalidating sales tax exemption for religious literature); Estate of Thornton v. Caldor, 472 U.S. 703 (1985) (invalidating law requiring employers to accommodate employees' Sabbath observance); Wallace v. Jaffree, 472 U.S. 38 (1985) (striking down law requiring public schools to allow students "moment of silence" for voluntary meditation or prayer).

27. *Cf.* Gerard V. Bradley, "The No Religious Test Clause and the Constitution of Religious Liberty: A Machine That Has Gone of Itself," 37 Case W. Res. L. Rev. 674, 734 (1987) ("[I]t is debatable whether the Supreme Court has contributed to or taken away from the present state of religious liberty — if indeed that describes the present state.").

28. *Id.* at 721–47.

29. Howe, *supra* note 1, at 174.

30. *Id.*

31. *Cf.* Gerard V. Bradley, "Protecting Religious Liberty: Judicial and Legislative Responsibilities," 42 DePaul L. Rev. 253, 260 (arguing that "we need to think about religious liberty free of the mental constraints that implicit commitments to judicial enforcement impose").

INDEX

and the religion question, 26–27, 38–39

"freedom of conscience" provisions, 40

fundamentalists
background beliefs of, 84
on evolution, 87

Gedicks, Frederick, on alienation through imposition of secularism, 117

"general goods," and common denominator approach, 88

Gey, Stephen, on religious authoritarianism, 102–03

Gibbon, Edward, 159–60 n.10

Glendon, Mary Ann, Raul Yanes
on Supreme Court failure to consider historical meaning of religion clauses, 4–5
and unitary conception of religion clauses, 37

governmental support of religion, 19–21, 26, 36–37, 105
in Massachusetts Constitution, 7
monetary, 37

Greenawalt, Kent, on common denominator approach to governmental neutrality, 88

Grove v. Mead School District, 85–86

Gunn, T. Jeremy, on singular purpose of religion clauses, 36

Harlan, Justice John Marshall, on neutrality, 78

Henry, Patrick, on support of religious freedom, 6

heretical position, 21

historical inquiry and historical view of religious freedom, 4, 5, 14, 46, 122–24

homogeneous community and civil strife, 109

Howe, Mark DeWolfe
on attempts to formulate principles, 120, 126–27
and dualistic view of religion clauses, 18

The Garden and the Wilderness, 18

imaginative reconstruction, 52

incorporation of religion clauses, 4, 18, 23, 35, 49, 50–54

Jackson, Justice Robert H., 9

Jefferson, Thomas
animus toward Christianity, 20
on blasphemy laws, 38
"Jeffersonian moment," 53
notion of separation, 54
opposition to Virginia assessments bill, 104
supporting religious freedom, 6
and Virginia Statute of Religious Freedom, 6, 8, 26, 46, 53
as a "voluntarist," 20

Johnson, Phillip, on neutrality, 77

judicial review
establishment of, 120–22
relinquishment of, 125–27

jurisdictional nature of religion clauses, 17–54

Karst, Kenneth, 139 n.3

Katz, Wilbur, on neutrality, 112–13

Kent, Chancellor, approving blasphemy prosecutions, 38

Kung, Hans, on trichotomy of values, 85

Kurland, Philip, on religious freedom and tolerance, 73–74

Lash, Kurt, on incorporation of religion clauses, 50–54

Laycock, Douglas
on constitutional principles, 7
on the establishment clause, 3, 31
on "substantive neutrality," 81

Lee v. Weisman, 3

legal positivism, 122–23

legal pragmatism, and doubts about legal theory, 61

legal realism, 55–57

legal scholarship, normative need in, 120–21

Leland, John, 53

Lemon test, 129 n.3
instability of, 3
secularism of, 81–82